D0065697

REDUCING
THE STORM
TO A WHISPER

REDUCING
THE STORM
TO A WHISPER

Patrick J. Howell, S.J.

THE THOMAS MORE PRESS
Chicago, Illinois

Grateful acknowledgment of permission to reprint:

From "Choruses from 'The Rock'" in COLLECTED
POEMS 1909-1962 by T.S. Eliot, copyright 1936 by
Harcourt Brace Jovanovich, Inc. copyright © 1963, 1964
by T.S. Eliot. Reprinted by permission of the publisher.

From "East Coker" in FOUR QUARTETS by T.S. Eliot,
copyright 1943 by T.S. Eliot; renewed 1971 by Esme
Valerie Eliot. Reprinted by permission of Harcourt Brace
Jovanovich, Inc.

Copyright © 1985 by Patrick J. Howell. All rights
reserved. Printed in the United States of America. No part
of this publication may be reproduced, stored in a retrieval
system, or transmitted, in any form or by any means,
electronic, mechanical, photocopying, recording, or
otherwise, without the written permission of the publisher,
The Thomas More Association, 223 W. Erie St., Chicago,
Illinois 60610.

ISBN 0-88347-183-3

616.89
H85r

88.2637

Contents

Psalm 107

He spoke and raised a gale,
lashing up towering waves.
Flung to the sky, then plunged to the depths,
they lost their nerve in the ordeal,
staggering and reeling like drunkards
with all their seamanship adrift.
Then they called to Yahweh in their trouble
and he rescued them from their sufferings,
reducing the storm to a whisper
until the waves grew quiet,
bringing them, glad at the calm,
safe to the port they were bound for.

The curious, the brave and the caring have asked me what my breakdown experience was like. I have dodged the questions, not because I wanted to, but because I could not spin a kaleidoscopic tale which would recreate the inner turmoil, the wild rage of fantasy and the whirling dread. Control had been such a paramount concern that I was acutely embarrassed to admit collapse. How easy it could happen! Who could understand? Who would listen? I myself did not grasp vast portions of this mad-house journey through the dark corridors of my mind.

Unlike Dante, I had no sure guide to begin this hellish search. My tattered mind, the light of reason was itself a geyser of fear. It was a source of illusions, misjudgments, and indecision. What was secure crumbled all around me. I resolved to plunge into this bewildering maelstrom. The darkness closed around me; wild, panoramic fears closed off the escape. I had first to live with the black night.

Introduction

THOUGH I struggled with my desire for anonymity, I decided a pseudonym would blur my own story about the breakdown I had in 1975. I preferred not to lacquer over what happened since direct communication and grappling with the real were the goals of my reintegration.

Even now, several years after the breakdown, I feel I am peering back through the haze of time and memory to meet myself, almost a stranger that I got to know rather well. Distance sifts out the peripheral and shapes the events and motivation even as I surge forward in uncharted paths to respond to the call to be more human.

This internal autobiography recounts the events of my life over a ten-year span from 1971 to 1981, from my last year in Rome before ordination to the end of my Jesuit tertianship, or final studies, which I made during my third year as principal at Gonzaga Prep in Spokane. I would much rather be reading this material about someone else since I find it unnerving to reveal my own innermost thoughts.

In the pivotal year of 1975 I considered that I was a well-integrated person with reasonable ambitions and a responsible job as principal of a boys' school of 520 students. I had good friends. I came from a solid family background with caring parents and a large family of nine brothers and sisters. I had entered the Jesuit order in 1961, enjoyed my many years of studies and training, and had begun to tackle some apostolic experiences as a young priest.

Then in the summer of 1975 I suffered a psychotic episode or breakdown. In one gulp I swallowed an ocean of images, emotions, and feelings. They swirled through all the regions of my being. This overwhelming storm within me galloped away and left me prostrate. The minimum period of recovery from this runaway tempest, I was told, was six months. I desperately hoped that I could resume my normal job as principal by then, and that the psychosis would not recur. Some psychotics, however, never recover. In fact until the advent of modern tranquilizers in 1953 the statistics were grim: about one-third returned to normalcy, one-third retained some psychotic symptoms, and about one-third became progressively worse after the first incident.

When first hospitalized, I was shocked at waking up to the screened windows and the stark, barren room. The raw, antiseptic smell of the hospital room put me in touch with my humanity in all its confusion, powerlessness, and abandonment. A numb fear gripped me. My psychosis had triggered an emotional explosion which destroyed my carefully constructed defenses.

Since I was a Jesuit priest and since my religious life was so much a part of me, this psychotic incident tore at the roots of my religious life. As a further complication, the psychosis began during my annual eight-day retreat, so my imagination and memory danced with religious imagery and ideas. The psychotic shock seared these images and ideas on my soul so that healing demanded religious as well as psychological medication; a spiritual reorientation would be the harbinger of a successful personal reintegration.

After a few years I gingerly touched on the painful experience and haltingly explained the events to a few close friends. Telling the story was itself part of the healing process, and like a multitextured history, a second, third or fourth narrative of the same material revealed facets that I had not noticed before. Each time I found the story shifted.

When I started to write the breakdown story, I tried to start from the beginning and to wind down through each experience in sequential order. This approach was tedious and largely fruitless except to put an artificial order on my disordered memories. So I have written these memories in a psychological rather than a strict chronological order. I circle round the memories and each time a new vista occurs; I catch a fleeting glance of myself in a rearview mirror.

During the first month in the hospital I conceived of the idea of keeping a diary of all the events which were occurring around me and to record my responses as well. I thought these reflections would make a good basis for a *Reader's Digest* article with which I could help pay my medical bills. The intention was noble but deluded, like a lot of my thinking at the time. Besides, I foundered in the inertia of failure which I felt to the marrow of my bones.

Visions are all misleading. How can anything be captured in this flux? I recalled my fifteenth year when my mother wanted me to publish a high-school essay in "Parade" magazine. Was I finally swallowing my anger at her for my rejection slip?

In the hospital I made a few notes and these were in fits and starts. Writing was a far too demanding task for a disintegrated mind. My mind floated through fantasies as bizarre as Coleridge's, but my imagination could not find the contours of time and discipline.

The impetus to delve into the past through storytelling came much later. Five of us Jesuits in Spokane began a prayer group in which I started to tell my story. The support of the groups helped me to face the past and to stretch myself over the broken pieces, much like a survivor of a sinking ship or war veteran retracing his harrowing experiences. I needed to tell the story over and over again, yet the images haunted me so that I was never finished with it: I circled my quarry as:

> On a huge hill,
> Craggy and steep, Truth stands and he that will
> Reach her, about must, and about must go.

I write this account for those who flounder in radical hopelessness, for the chronically ill, that they may see a glimmer of light. I write this internal journey especially for my brother Jesuits and other men and women religious because I believe that this story of a faith experience dives to the roots of religious life and our participation in the *kenosis,* the Pauline emptying out and groping for our humanity. The final im-

petus for writing this account was the realization after conversations with fellow Jesuits that many could relate a similar
faith history, an account of the intimate experience of God
touching and working at the core of one's being and personal
history. At the same time I realized that many of my other
fellow priests and religious suffered from psychosomatic ill-
nesses, such as early heart attacks, severe tension, ulcers,
alcoholism, and the like—fundamentally psychological problems, and often religious problems as well.

This enterprise would not have been possible without some
crucial, caring people. My gratitude to my parents, who will
no doubt read parts of this book with pain and anguish, is
immense. I trust because of their abiding love they will be
pleased with the results. My eight brothers and sisters are also
a vital and supportive cast.

The doctor assisting at my second birth was Dr. William
Zieverink, director of psychiatric services at Providence
Medical Center in Portland, Oregon. My psychiatrist for two
years, he nurtured my psyche, challenged my paralyzing
assumptions, and invited me to grow. He urged that the most
enterprising and far-reaching task I could undertake was to
work through my own crippling projections in order to attain
the freedom of being a whole person on all the levels of the
physical, social, psychological, and spiritual. In addition, he
was most generous in encouraging this book once I had
stumbled onto it.

Finally, this autobiographical account of an inward
journey would be unfinished and distorted without the inclu-
sion of my Jesuit family. I am grateful to my many Jesuit
brothers who supported me with their prayers and compassion. I am particularly grateful to those with whom I have
struggled in one way or another through my relationships.
Special thanks to my communities at the Gesù (Rome), Jesuit
High School (Portland, Oregon), Gonzaga Prep (Spokane)
and to my retreat directors. Those who saw me through the

darkest hours with their care and friendship were Robert Byrne, Kevin Clarke, Jim McDonough, Mike Merriman, and Steve Sundborg. Steve Kuder, my literary therapist, yielded up his reserve of incisive criticism and editorial skill with generosity and wit, and Donald Campion sheered away my verbiage with such ease that I was almost delighted.

I suspect that at least my friends and family will find what's not said as interesting as what is revealed at length. Any spiritual journey is ultimately masked by privacy and revealed in intimacy. Writing an interior autobiography should be reserved for septuagenarians who have sifted wisdom and desire, love and memory, and know the difference. Yet my mid-age indiscretion may give some courage to those who endure their own murky journey now and cannot wait 30 years for another's confessional witness.

August 1983
Spokane, Washington

December 1982

Usually the school has slowed down to a normal pace by now, but since we won the semifinal game against Bellarmine yesterday, we will be headed to the Kingdome in Seattle next weekend. I'll have to plot out the transportation and logistics of getting 600 students, the football team, the cheerleaders and the rowdy boosters to Seattle. The phone will be ringing off the hook on Monday with sky-high fans queuing up for tickets.

My friend and editor, Kuder, suggested looking at Dante since he wrote an interior journey. The Commedia makes more sense now than it did when I read it with Doc Schneider at Gonzaga University 24 years ago: "Mid-way through life I found myself in a dark mood." Dante was 35 when he wrote his epic.

A healing story would normally end in thanksgiving, an openness to the mystery of life within and beyond oneself. My story is more pedestrian; it needs to be in touch with people, with myself. The psychotic is out of touch with the world, needs to cling to every smidgeon he can find. It would not be a healing story unless someone had brought me down to earth, forced me to traverse the finite and the real.

My memory plays tricks on me. Casting a glance to the past, I catch myself in a mirror then another mirror, and another and finally a reflection in the mirror from another mirror. The images cascade about. Which perspective tells the truth? To begin the journey, Kuder says: "Set up that ladder where all ladders start—in the foul rag and bone shop of the heart."

Chapter One
THEOLOGY IN ROME

April, 1971 Rome

The prologue to my breakdown occurred in my days of theology in Rome, the year I made my first directed retreat. Rome, the crossroads of the Mediterranean, burgeons with a carnival atmosphere. The honking traffic, the frantic gestures and the hawking of flowers and roasted chestnuts rarely cease, except during the World Cup soccer matches when all the Romans are glued to their TV sets. Rome pulses with excitement and the monumental past clashes with the urgency of the present. After two years in Rome, I was beginning to laugh less at the old joke: Rome was the "city of faith" because so many of the faithful had come there, lost their faith and left it behind. Theology classes were as solid, and dull, as the grayish marble piles within which a staid faculty taught. When the faculty shifted from Latin to Italian for teaching in 1969, the pedagogy made a great leap forward and landed in about the 17th century. The Latin notes were now translated, but still in the same sterile, ecclesiastical idioms.

When I arrived in 1969, just four years after the Second Vatican Council, the electricity from the reforms was still in the air. Priests and religious were no longer bound by curfews and required relgious garb. The church had burst its bonds to the 16th century and opened its doors to the culture of Asia and Africa; "church" was no longer static and one, but mobile and diverse. Since the seminarians at the "Greg," as we referred to the university, were from over 100 countries, a vibrant group of intelligent, questioning students was created. At the Greg, bank after bank of cramped writing desks surrounded the magisterial podium. In a concession to modernity, the professor used a microphone to project his voice to the black-and-gray-garbed students who scribbled away. Some classes held up to 400 students. The medieval-style lectures were a barrier, but the international perspective of both students and faculty nearly compensated for the quaint pedagogy. Despite a heavy reliance on French and German theology, a "Common Market" bias, the strength of the university lay in teaching the tradition and continuity of theology. One student said: "In the last ten years every professor has written or read a book." The same quip has since been applied to many other faculties.

Many Gregorian University professors were struggling valiantly to stay abreast of all the changes, as well as to suggest avenues for the future. Many of the teachers had been *periti* or special advisers at the Council, so they were charged up with what had happened, although their energy lost some of its zip in the classroom. They were scrambling to incorporate the latest thinking of the church which had emerged from the key documents of Vatican II. Some were rewriting their notes, but most of what they wrote was predictable.

I lived at the Collegio Internazionale del Gesù, a 350-year-old edifice that Cardinal Farnese built for his Jesuit friends on the same location as the original three houses bought by St. Ignatius for the General Curia, or Jesuit headquarters. The Gesù community hosted Venezuelans, Americans, Ruwandans, Italians, Spaniards, a Belgian, a Philippino, a Frenchman; in short, an international band of Jesuits. Typical of the seminaries in Rome, the hallways were drafty, massive and lined with marble. The elegant refectory, the scene of the Brief of Suppression of the Society in 1773, was leased to a rug shop. For eating, the scholastics were confined to a narrow corridor which lined the inner courtyard. Rather than boasting the palm trees and potted plants that bedecked most inner courtyards, ours had been paved over to provide a makeshift basketball court.

Italian, the house language, came readily for most, especially the Spaniards who learned about 50 words of

Italian and then rattled through the language. Fortunately the Italians were patient mentors, not at all touchy about our massacring the *bella lingua*. Fr. Pedro Arrupe, the Jesuit Superior General, would visit the Gesù, which he affectionately dubbed "his theologate," and would give his own light-hearted rendition of Basque songs. Many of the more memorable occasions were the song fests with contributions from the 21 countries represented.

These were the surface impressions. On a deeper level my psyche was not nearly so peaceful, though I was unaware of any difficulties and the chest constrictions which I experienced periodically proved to be nothing when I checked things out with a local Polish doctor who had lived in Rome for 30 years.

My personal religious disposition was basically mercantile spirituality: *do ut des*. Give in order to receive. I was earning perfection, as if God's love could be bought. I said to a Jesuit friend during a moment of discouragement: "You do what you can, and it's never enough." He exclaimed: "You do what you can, and that's plenty!"

One event traumatized me for about a week. In those years a shift was occurring from the old "black-box" style confessional to a more personal, face-to-face encounter. I did not make the change-over gracefully. Nor did I not know any priest well enough to feel comfortable face to face; I was still a highly private person. As a result I went for some 17 months without going to confession. The longer the delay, the guiltier I felt for letting it drag on. Our Jesuit "rule" said to go once a week although every couple of months was becoming more common. Finally I resolved to walk the four miles over to St. Peter's at the Vatican where there were plenty of anonymous English-speaking confessors in the old-style confessional. I walked up the grand entrance of St. Peter's flanked by Bernini's embracing columns and entered the tourist-filled church. I had been here many times and knew my way. I wandered over the inlaid marble floors up to the baldichinoed altar and turning off to the left entered with trepidation a confessional that said "English/German." I blessed myself and said: "I'm a seminarian; it's been 17 months since my last confession." There was an uproar from the other side, and tremulously I explained or tried to explain why it had been so long and my difficulties with the style of confession, especially in a foreign country. The priest was in such a rage that I had a difficult time thinking clearly.

I am not certain the priest heard what I had to confess, and I certainly do not remember it. At the end I said I was sorry for all my sins and awaited the penance. He said: "For your penance say the rosary every day for 30 days!" I felt angry and then shook all over when I heard myself say: "I think that's excessive and I can't accept the penance." With that he said: "Then I can't give you absolution!" and closed the curtain. I was stunned and wandered out into the bright Sunday morning, barely hearing the shrill pealing of the bells; I was numb at not being understood and trembled at my audacity.

A week later a priest from Detroit whom I knew rather well arrived at the Gesù for some extended research at the Vatican. Each evening seven of us Americans would gather round a small table as he celebrated a refreshingly simple Eucharist. Still in a turmoil about my encounter with the raging priest in the confessional, I looked for the right moment to approach this congenial Jesuit. Finally after a couple of agonizing days, I knocked on his door, once more asked to go to confession, and started in. He glanced off to the side as if he did not want to interrupt my pain or to heighten my embarrassment. When I finished, he reassured me about my refusing the penance and was vehement about the Vatican confessor: "The man should be denounced to the Holy See and removed from the confessional." I was taken aback at the force of his anger and did not want to become embroiled any further in Vatican ways. I was silently relieved that I did not remember seeing any name on the confessional door.

We chatted peacefully for several minutes. My shattered soul was on the mend. What did not emerge was how I had fallen into this labyrinthian way. This grotesque episode stirred my compassion in my own role as a confessor. I recall some years after I was ordained hearing a confession that started: "Father it's been 48 years since my last confession. I don't know where to start." Knowing the feeling, I said: "Welcome back! Let me see if I can help you."

During my second semester of my second year at the Gregorian, I had been elected president of the student body within the theology faculty, and so was embroiled in the inevitable confrontation and machinations of an extremely complicated university political situation. Diplomacy and precisely nuanced language were needed. I still spoke only a rough-hewn Italian. I clashed with the Dean on revisions in the academic policies; then tempers flared when several students staged a demonstration against the hike in tuition. It had been raised from $85 to $115 per year, hardly significant from an American point of view, but the sit-in in the stately inner court enraged some faculty members. One professor wanted to bring in the firemen to hose down the students.

I was impatient with centuries of sluggishness. So although my natural political instincts were moderate to conservative, I found that in Rome I had to be radical to be centrist enough to budge anything. By the end of 1971, I felt a shallowness in my spiritual life and a lack of direction. I realized I needed a directed retreat; I also needed a break from Rome.

Rather weary, I returned to the USA in June with a stop-over in New York. I observed the garish clothes, the people bulky from overeating and the incredible sprawling highway system. Everything seemed expansive and overdone. Having landed on Father's Day, I watched a large family of parents, children and grandparents celebrate an American-style Father's Day in the airport restaurant. As I sat off to the side nibbling some toast, I felt like a foreign observer. The grand-

father was the center of attention. Waitresses, dressed in stiff
tight-fitting uniforms, brought several rounds of ham, bacon, orange juice, eggs and cinnamon rolls. What a contrast
to our Italian breakfast of steamed milk and coffee and a dry
roll with marmalade. As the meal progressed, the gathering
picked up volume and verve. Finally ribboned packages
sprang from nowhere, admidst smiles, laughter and thank
you's. A pile of gifts and wrapping paper filled the table and
spilled out round about them. I finished my simple breakfast,
breathed deeply and looked forward to catching my flight
back to North Dakota.

I spent a week at home in Lisbon, N.D., where we
celebrated my sister Margaret's wedding. Margaret was only
seven years younger than I and because of all our kidding
back and forth and our responsibility of being the oldest boy
and the oldest girl in a family of nine children, we were very
close to each other. She had visited me in Rome two years before with a couple of friends. I recalled how we took the bus
to St. Peter's and how I chuckled over her consternation
when I asked her if she had her passport to enter the Vatican,
a foreign country. Tom, her husband, was a strapping, sharp
farmer who had his degree in agriculture from North Dakota
State. He and my dad became fast friends in endless conversations over the state of the nation, business, and farming.
The wedding events culminated in a traditional wedding
dance which was *de rigueur* for our family. As I danced with
Margaret she reminded me that I had once called her
"sixteen-ton," when she was a slender sixth grader. "I was
convinced I would be a fat blimp the rest of my life," she said
in her soft North Dakota drawl.

We did not have much time to reminisce; her other five
brothers were queued up behind me.

After a restful summer in Portland, Oregon, I made a
directed retreat at my old novitiate at Sheridan, Oregon. The
brick building was perched high up in the parched hills of the
Yamhill valley. In summer the normally lush grass, hoary oak

trees, and myriad rivulets shriveled; cricket-filled cracks seamed the land.

Until 1970 my experience of retreats had been the old-fashioned kind: the priest gave a half-hour talk four times a day, and personal prayer was squeezed in between. Most of us had complained about the lengthy, often canned talks, but no one challenged the system. The change in retreats came as we returned to our roots and to the charisma of the founder, as Vatican II suggested. St. Ignatius had meant *The Spiritual Exercises* to be given individually, not in large, impersonal groups. Thus individually directed retreats received new impetus shortly after Vatican II. The Ignatian ideal of allowing the Spirit to work in the individual's life and of helping the retreatant to realize how and where the Spirit was leading gradually took root again.

I was apprehensive about talking to someone else about my personal prayer life, probably because I felt that I had to be a spiritual giant on prayer by now. My previous experience with spiritual directors had been largely negative. I would leave a spiritual-direction session with a feeling of depression, or, in a few positive moments, with a sense of superficiality. I wanted to be honest, but I skimmed the surface. No real probing occurred and the session would not make much difference. I went out of duty, rather than with any relish or sense of progress.

I remember feeling good about my first directed retreat because I was honest with my director, Bill, and he kept up his end of the chatter. In fact, he had brought with him an incredible green parrot with red markings. When all else failed, he would banter with the parrot: "What do you think, Polly?" And then interpret her squawk. In a homily Bill spoke of how the Lord calls us to realize our own deepest potential of "letting free the eagle within you!" As I sought to verbalize my own obscure emotions, I thought of that ridiculous parrot and suddenly got the idea.

Christ was a model but not a person to me. He was too

abstract. I prayed to the Father. Love that is a commitment
to a human person was missing. For me God was a lawgiver
with a fixed will which I needed to discover. If I could tap
into wherever God was, then I could find out what I was supposed to do. My mechanistic view of God underlay my assessment of myself. In William Blatty's novel *The Exorcist* the
devil's message is: "You're no damn good." The call of
Christ reverses this: He calls me by name instead of names.
He could help me to realize my basic goodness.

On the plane flying back to Rome, I was thankful that I
had not felt compelled to meet performance standards during
the retreat. The apostle feels a movement of interior revolt at
the Passion. Suffering is the underside of glory. I gazed out
the window to the surging ocean below. Like Peter, I am
sleepy, impetuous, self-indulgent and unable to follow
through to the finish. Thank God for Bill and his crazy parrot. He carried a hazel twig to divine any hidden spring.
Maybe now I could hang less on authority figures to seek
their approval.

When I arrived in Rome, the baggage handlers were on
strike. In pouring rain all the passengers circled round the
luggage wagons to retrieve their bags. I knew I was back to
the carnival. The third and final year of theology was quieter,
more reflective. I disengaged politically and had time for a
wide range of reading in theology. An article in *Theological
Studies* in the winter of 1971 by John O'Malley made a strong
impact on me. Its thesis was that Vatican II's reforms could
not be understood in the traditional fashion as a correction or
revival or development or even an updating. The Council's
reforms, he said, were a transformation, a revolution, which
involved creativity; and creativity means something new—in
part at least, a rejection of the past. The Catholic cultural
ghetto which existed in part until 1962 had to be terminated
and a new attitude towards the "world" had to be assumed.

O'Malley quoted his old friend Giles of Viterbo at the Fifth Lateran Council: "Men must be changed by religion, not religion by men." For the first time Vatican II, however, was saying the opposite. Religion must be changed by men and women so that they could worship God from the wealth of their own experience.

My own personal life was barely beginning to shift; at least the changes had not registered yet. I was still trapped by my personal history which I viewed uncritically and naively. The mythic power of my own past dominated me; likewise, my views of the church needed to be demythologized so that I could respond to my own vocation and to the needs of others with fidelity and freedom.

December, 1982

No, Kuder, I don't think Rome is a symbol of anything in particular. Perhaps "Aida" in the Baths of Caracalla, a splendid opera with chariots, elephants and a grand troupe performed in mid-summer in the open air best captures the carnival of Rome. Or maybe it's "Il Papa," the Pope, praying the Angelus on a Sunday at St. Peter's piazza and blessing the eager throng waving bandiere, handkerchiefs, rosaries and veils.

My favorite image of Rome is Piazza Navona on a quiet dusk-blue night. Built on the old Domitian stadium, the piazza revolves about Bernini's four rivers, the central fountain. The overflowing baroque style entwines and overpowers the more rigorous classical manner of the ancient city. It's the people, though, that make the place: parents tugging bambini by the hand, slim artists vending their garret creations, and seminarians jostling with the natives for "un gelato misto," a multiflavored ice cream cone. I finally found just what I wanted at Navona among the many paintings that the young, eager artists offered for sale: an oil painting of the Roman Forum, splendid among the ruined columns and strewn stones, overgrown with vines and bushes pushing up through the broken pavement. I gave it to my folks for Christmas.

Chapter Two
ROME—ORDINATION RETREAT

In March, 1972, twelve of us *ordinandi* (those to be ordained) from the Gesù made an ordination retreat at Galloro, the old Jesuit novitiate in the Frascati hills, about 30 kilometers from Rome. As we climbed up through the hillside in a bus, a warm spring air touched each of us, stirred up a riot of swallows and bursting buds.

The Roman novitiate, a short way from Pope Paul VI's summer residence at Castel Gandolfo, gave us a hollow welcome. A gnarled vine clung to the gray red facade on the right of the manor door. No one our age was in sight. There to meet us was the superior clad in a musty cassock. A few ancient Jesuits shuffled around through the echoing hallways. As in many European Jesuit homes, I was a little hesitant to inquire what anyone did. It was often as marginal as "running a boys' club for teenagers." Earlier novitiates had been bustling with activity. This one was stone still. In all of Italy, which was already experiencing a shortage of young priests, there were only five or six Jesuit novices. This scarcity was a harbinger, I thought, of what faced us in all parts of the Society of Jesus in 20 years. Shakespeare's sonnet, "Bare ruined choirs, where late the sweet birds sang," echoed through my head. This empty building was the uneasy context of my ordination retreat. My hopes lay more in the small groups of Jesuit friends who remained, not in the expansive and vibrant numbers of an earlier Society.

Our director, Federico Arvesu, was himself a survivor. About 50, he had been provincial of Cuba after the Jesuits fled from the Castro takeover in 1961. The Jesuits resettled all over the Caribbean, especially in Miami and the Dominican Republic. The wrenching had left scars on our director which he rarely touched on.

Arvesu sagely suggested a retreat "di gruppo" in which we
shared our retreat experiences in a group. He said: "Interaction is not important at first. What is crucial is to share the
fruit of your own prayer." That evening before the late
Italian supper, we had a further discussion and discerned
with Arvesu the directions of our prayer for the next day, a
pattern we held to each day. As Roby, a vibrant Northern
Italian spoke, I found my own inarticulate prayer experience
shaped and formulated. When Eduardo, a serious Cuban,
said he was confused and his prayer was arid, I could see my
own obstacles more clearly because of his openness about his
own defenses. Listening to others thus became a central part
of the retreat.

Gradually we built each other up by our mutual support,
and I could sense God's work in the group. At the beginning
the direction was unclear, especially since each one was giving
his own prayer reflections without attempting to tie them in
with what anyone else in the group had said.

Conversion or *metanoia* was one of the first themes we
selected. I was struck by a comment by Ramon, a swarthy
Brazilian: "Idols in my life are a need for human security.
Conversion consists in a correspondence between my own self
realization and God's plan. There is a tension between my
clinging to my own human security and God's plan for me."
A vague fear stirred within me. I clung unconsciously to my
roots. Paolo, another spirited Brazilian, said: "God accepts
us as we are, so our conversion consists in accepting ourselves
as he accepts us."

I heard Sergio, a lean Venetian, saying: "Conversion is
frightening. I fear taking faith too seriously, lest I be naked
before God." I was not at all ready for stripping away my
psychological defenses although I could see that the reflections of the group unearthed some of my deeper obstacles to
God's working in me.

At the end of the discernment phase, Arvesu swiftly underlined a few key insights. He said the opening to the Spirit is a

complicated feat. We want to be worthy to be loved, so we seek to prove ourselves. We do not want to place ourselves on the block because of egotism. We cling to our defenses and are haunted by them. But our own witnessing gives others the experience of God. If I can freely witness to God's action in me, then I free others to do the same.

Conversion was not a new theme for me. I found it a daily requirement, though I usually burrowed down into my own ways and habits and resisted change. Like the apostles going about their fishing; I was comfortable, though yearning vaguely for something better, and above all safe.

That afternoon I walked down the old highway, probably a footpath in Roman times, through the Alban hills. Verdant bushes had a tinge of spring, the delicate yellow green of new life. About two miles away I wandered through a village, unchanged in 400 years, maybe more. Three women were washing laundry in an ancient, open-air trough close by the central piazza. Young boys scampered around kicking a soccer ball in the narrow street, and the village elders caught the sun on the shabby chairs among the tables in front of the only *ristorante*.

I kicked a stone and mused: was conversion confused with social change in the modern era of rapid industrialization and political upheaval? Why upset this charming, antiquated village? Certainly this rural village expected a tamer style of change. Very little changed here and very little would change. I was confused. Personal conversion seemed so radical, and I was unprepared to uproot my cherished defenses. Why destroy a harmonious pattern of life?

A couple of days later we were considering the theme of "A priest, a man of love." Again we shared our reflections in the group. Roby, my Italian friend, said: "To be a priest is to walk with men. We need to experience our humanity and frailty, our doubts and probing for answers so that we can respond to the needs of others."

"Pat, you always want things perfect. You'll have to live

*with a little failure. It's not the end of the world because you
weren't elected." I could hear my mother's sympathetic voice
encouraging me, trying to chip away at my importance.
"That's fine for you to say, but you'd be the same way.
How'd you feel when you didn't get that part in the play!"*

Paolo of Brazil had a striking image of the sterile priest
who is devoid of a strong affective life. He said: "What does
it mean to be a loving priest? We live in a very masculine
church. One priest I know was a porcupine with women, but
after a few years he lost his quills! On the other hand, we
can't be Don Juan's."

Arvesu underlined the importance of generosity. God has
shown each of us what it means to be generous. We too need
to take the first step in love since you learn love only by loving.
In this you cannot avoid conflicts which will inevitably come,
but a person who loves will be able to face conflict, struggle
with it and grow from it. Our celibate life is impossible without
a strong affective prayer life and personal relationships.

That afternoon I strolled through the backyard bordered
by trellises covered with new vines. The young sprouts were
strewn every which way. At the end of the garden walks
where the novices used to say the rosary was the hog shed.
The cooks slopped the pigs there twice a day. Loud squeals
peeled through the quiet walks and vines. Honey bees flitted
through the arbor and hovered over the vineyard. In the glow
of the spring sun, random thoughts floated, settled and
escaped: "I am the vine, you are the branches." Friendship
with the Lord can be very intimate. It is an invitation I have
not accepted, I have not been able to accept. I usually pray to
the Father, not to the Son, not to Christ. Christ is an abstrac-
tion, a historical figure. I sense he is there but distant. I admire him, I would like to know him better, but he is on a
different level from me. I could never be a friend because we
are so unequal.

In the next group session the energetic Paolo said: "The

church is no longer a perfect society, the old model of the church; now it is the People of God. The priest, therefore, is no longer a prince, but a pilgrim walking alongside the people." The stability of the old church had crumbled. It was no longer a self-contained society, but rather a people on the move, walking with and towards the Lord.

Afterwards, as I was praying in the chapel, I felt some glimmer of the glory of God. A vision of a shower of pink camilla blossoms spilling from the sky came to me. It was a brief, intense moment, like a whiff of a rare perfume. My chest burned with joy. Later in the group I had to explain it as a rain of roses, *pioggia di rose,* because I did not know the right Italian words.

I knew the group was energized by what I said as if the tongues of flame were descending on each of us, then drawing us to a unity in one constant flame. We drove each other on as the flames in a forest fire lap at each other's heels long after the wind has died down.

That night at dinner Beethoven's *Ninth Symphony* was playing in the background. I did not notice the food. The "Ode to Joy" was an analogue for me of my rushing feelings of joy. Each instrument and voice in the symphony was an individual hymn playing its part in praising the Lord. All joined in a common chorus. Our group too was a symphonic choir doubling and redoubling joy and glory.

The next day our group was desolate. "My prayer was flat," someone said. Another added: "All I can think about is all the work I have to do on papers next week." I said: "The call of Moses to lead his people out of Egypt was ratified long after the Exodus. Our vocation is a call authenticated by its living out. It's a long, hard grind." Uncertainty of the future, fear of how our priesthood would take root, dread of failure gripped us. Miguel of Spain mentioned that Ananias in the Acts of the Apostles, representing the official church, also experienced doubt in accepting the renegade Paul.

The director Arvesu said: "Desolation indicates an obstacle to the Spirit. There can be too much apprehension about the future." He gave a personal example: "I was told when I started theology at Frankfurt that to finish the four years I would need to eat 50 kilometers of wurst!" "You see," he said, "priesthood needs to be lived day to day. Do not compound the fears by compressing them all together."

Towards the end of the retreat I felt a lot of distractions and tensions during prayer. I realized I was trying to overachieve by forcing an attitude of prayerfulness. I was called back to a realization that Rome was not built in a day. Love is a process of day-by-day growth.

The final day was a culmination of many thoughts on the priesthood and a strong convergence in the group on the experiences of the retreat. That evening in my ill-lit, high-ceilinged, white-washed room, I jotted down some ideas:

The priest's serenity and confidence is not to be found in human things, but sought in the Holy Spirit. For instance, in Exodus when God appears to Moses, he does not promise success itself, only "I will be with you." Our need for success is not the Lord's. In fact, the exodus and the cross point to a long human struggle. I would not realize the depth of this struggle until many years later.

Our group is a micro-church and an image of the Society of Jesus. Through interaction with others, the priest realizes he is never fully integrated. He has to be open to the Spirit to seek where he (we) should go. He never has it made. The call beckons beyond all security. Hence conversion is a daily need. I could start to step out of my hidebound security because of the support of our group. I found *gusto* in prayer, community, priesthood and friendship.

I recalled what Ramon from Brazil said this afternoon: "I was in the garden; I sat down under the vines. I stopped to hear Jos singing. Flowers were opening in the garden. All was bursting with new life, yet our own life is even greater. Then I thought of those fantastic roses of Pat's. The Holy Spirit gives in great abundance. The Spirit is truly in everyone and wherever there exists peace, joy and beauty. Just as I was leaning back and praying over all these ideas, my chair tipped and I fell over backwards onto the ground. Such somersaults re-orientate one's whole life.''

I felt that the action of the Spirit is not tranquil. But we lead lives of hope which is already active. Everything counts in our lives—our failures, distractions, suffering and joy. All work together unto good and to God.

I contrasted this with the demonic spirit which suggests identification with failure. "You're no damn good," is the evil spirit's subtle lie, and he catches us at our most vulnerable spot, whatever that is.

When I wrote all this, I felt a certain heaviness. Instead of experiencing joy at tremendous graces received during the retreat, I was saddened by my own failures. I sensed: "I have so far to go, so many things to do, it seems overwhelming.''

When we returned to Rome, we had ordinations to the diaconate in the splendid baroque Church of the Gesù. Bishop Paul Marcinkus, the new president of the Vatican Bank, ordained us.

During the diaconate ordination I felt a surge of strength when I said: "I am ready and willing.'' Being ordained with close friends for these years and confreres on the retreat was also a source of strength. At the reception in the Jesuit recreation room, the former site of Jesuit General Congregations, enthusiastic Jesuit seminarians spilled out all over, then huddled in masses and rocked with laughter. It was still Lent and I had made a bet with Steve Sundborg, an American Jesuit friend, that he could not give up smoking until Easter. I spotted him halfway across the densely packed room. He was gesturing in a smoker's fit and pleading for a one-day respite. Calculating it would be more difficult for him to go back to abstinence again, I granted it with great largesse.

Shortly after the ordination, my mother, my brother Mike and his wife Kela arrived in Rome. We took a whirlwind tour of Rome, Pompeii, Florence and Venice. My father had decided to stay home in North Dakota since he did not like hoofing it around to all the sights, although he said: "I'd just as soon be there for the parties at night."

Among the many sights, we attended an audience of Paul VI in the new audience hall to the south of St. Peter's Basilica. The crowd was huge, but Paul personalized it by speaking affectionately to many different groups. My image of him was of a kindly Italian grandfather, not the stern, anxious scholar so often portrayed in the media. We enjoyed the carnival atmosphere of Rome, the ghostly ruins at ancient Pompeii—even in the rain—and the bustling bazaar in Florence. Soon I was bidding the three of them farewell from a train station in Venice before they flew off to London.

It was a beautiful spring in Rome.

After the ordinations I spent about ten days reflecting on the retreat experiences, writing copious notes and conferring with Arvesu. I looked back on this retreat as a transforming experience. I had a glimmer of the Lord's numinous presence and had few ways to express the experience. In fact, the image of the "roses" and other symbols, such as music and community, were an integral part of the experience. These diaphanous symbols made palpable the Lord's presence and were types of revelation.

I kept pondering inspirations from the retreat. Like a first encounter with a wonderful person, I traced the new images of the Lord through my thoughts and feelings in order to grasp what had happened. I was at peace, but unsettled. I had stretched a bit, but I was still firmly anchored to my tried-and-true ways. A desire for some kind of personal glory was a strong element. My self-esteem, ironically, was low; I sought approval from others to bolster my ego. Much of this became clear only in hindsight after my psychotic somersault three years later.

In order to sort through my inchoate spiritual yearnings, I made sporadic jottings in a diary. On May 7, 1972, I wrote: "I wonder if most people do not learn prayer because they are forced to pray. They reach a crisis point in their lives. At that point they can either follow a destructive, mindless path or they can begin to recreate themselves, hand in hand with the Creator. Death, sickness, marriage, ordination and so forth, focus our frailty." The moorings to my Law Giver were unraveling. A God who was present only in sickness and death was unjust. Yet the Mystery was larger than this.

I was stretching out of my narrow confines without knowing it. My careful, but knowing friend, Steve, said: "Don't restrict the expansiveness of God's love and freedom. God acts in every situation." I said: "It sounds like Job's discovery." God touches him in his anguish, his challenge and his suffering. Job's friends try to rationalize God into human components. Job knows the Mystery is greater:

> All this but skirts the ways he treads,
> A whispered echo is all that we hear of him.
> But who could comprehend the thunder of his power?
>> Job 26:14

I concluded my stay in Rome with a toss of a coin in the Trevi fountain and one final entry on June 16, 1972: "Fear flourishes in the pursuit of honor, love and faith. In honor because we fear defeat, in love because we fear rejection, in faith because we fear the loss of self." Or does fear wear two masks—one which leads to success, the other to failure. The one creates energy, spark and wit; the other tensions, anxiety and withdrawal. Unfortunately for me the latter was to become more and more prevalent.

December, 1982

Coming home was like a wild dream; we breezed up into the snow-capped mountains where the rain had been cascading a few days before. We left the dome in a frenzied, exhausted mood. No, not Rome. The dome. The Kingdome. We beat South Kitsap 25-7, the biggest upset in the history of football playoffs. The kids said, "We were awesome." The papers were full of long pictorial spreads for three days.

Rome was that way too: a constant festival. It evoked monumental, trick mirror fantasies.

Kuder again: "The thought occurs that your father is really mentioned for the first time here; he becomes central to your recovery period. Is his absence from the trip to Rome somehow a foreshadowing?" Kuder and Fellini ought to meet someday. They could regale each other with their rapid-fire imaginations. Perhaps when I wrote this, Dad's absence from those festive days was a symbol for my longing for him to be there just when I was stretching my wings towards ordination. No, I did not think of that at the time. I know he would have enjoyed the wine and cheese and dark Italian breads. Mother, Mike, Kela and I had an exotic cheese dip with bologna one night in Florence; we kept saying how much he would have enjoyed it all.

Chapter Three
PRIESTHOOD 1972 - 1975

A week later I left by train with two other Jesuits for Brindisi on the Italian east coast. It was a jump-off point for Athens and a six-week tour of the Middle East and the Holy Land, the final cap on my preparation for ordination in my home town of Lisbon, North Dakota, on August 19. This Middle East trip advanced my thoughts from the retreat. When I visited the ancient religious sites—Mythraic, Canaanite, Christian, Byzantine, Moslem—I often sensed a sacred presence that transcended the passing centuries.

Jerusalem stood like a jewel bedecked with silver domes, mosques, and church bells. I trod the path of Jesus up the Kidron Valley towards the Golden Gate. Odors of mules, fresh vegetables and exotic, musty spices mingled in the dense Arab streets. The Israeli takeover was just beginning: each side was testing the other, jabbing here and there to probe the sore spots. Young John the disciple had raced through these narrow streets fighting the surging crowds and tensing his emotions as he searched for Jesus, finally had found him in Pilate's courtyard down the street from where I stood. In a week I would be ordained in a far-off land with a feast more like the simple wedding feast of Cana with family, friends, song and dance. A throaty Arab voice alongside me startled me out of my reverie.

On a clear Sunday morning I boarded a rickety bus to Tel Aviv, flew to Paris, did a whirlwind, one-day tour of Paris with Steve as preplanned, then plunged on into the starry night for the journey to Fargo.

My mother was relieved to see me; she knew how to run a wedding, but an ordination was beyond her scope. Together we plotted out the week; she took charge of all the food, reception, party and dance. Her confidence restored, she assembled her command post and started directing the family. I worked out a simple ordination liturgy. Bishop Driscoll of Fargo, a formal but friendly man, had agreed to do the ordination in my home town, a departure from the usual ordinations in the Bishop's cathedral. Four other Jesuits from the Oregon province drove or flew out to North Dakota for the celebration: two of them from Jesuit High, one from Portland and one from Missoula. My eight brothers and sisters, a swath of my 50 first cousins and a broad sweep of the town itself turned out to rejoice and celebrate.

I walked down the aisle of the crowded church with my mother and father on either side. We stood together in the front pew until I was called forth for the ordination. As was traditional, the congregation clapped loudly when I was accepted for ordination by the Bishop. With a brief imposition of hands I joined the long line of priests extending through the ages to the apostles. Tom Holden, a Jesuit from Chicago who was a classmate in Rome, vested me for Mass. I wore a golden chasuble with blue markings, one that for years had been reserved for the most solemn Masses in the church. I recalled Monsignor O'Donoghue wearing it when I served his Christmas Mass 20 years before. After the Mass the long day of celebration began. My dad had an open bar in our back yard for several hundred people. He was surprised at the end of the party when he counted as many full bottles as he had started with. Friends had brought donations to round out the supply. Dad said: "It's really not that difficult to change water into wine."

That evening we had a dinner in the parish hall, concluded by outrageous skits by my uninhibited relatives. Three of my aunts dressed up as Parisian ladies of the night, women of my checkered past, traipsed around the tables in a seductive fashion. My Mikkelson uncles sang the "Farmers' Union Song," followed by my sister Ginny belting out "Squaws Along the Yukon." The entertainment lasted for a couple of hours until we broke up for the ordination dance at a dance hall north of town. It was a hot, muggy, bug-ridden night so the dancers were pouring sweat; the heat did not slow the party one iota. The exuberance lasted well after midnight when I returned home to write my homily for my First Mass the next morning at 10 o'clock and to recuperate. Fatigue, rather than prudence, slowed down the continuing celebration. I remember celebrating my First Mass more from the pictures my uncle Tom took than from the event itself.

After the heat the rains came and the crowd dispersed. The Reynolds cousins headed back for Illinois; my brother Tom headed out West; many of us drove in the torrential rain to Detroit Lakes, Minnesota, for a short two-day break. Immediately after I was rushing out to Portland to learn the ropes of my new job as academic vice principal. I arrived at Jesuit High about a week before school started. I expected a hectic beginning; which it was. A new office was being built for me, so to escape the confusion I sped down to the Oregon Coast for a break before the excitement began.

As I gazed at the frothy waves, my thoughts probed across the horizon for the source of the endless, rolling, thunderous waves. Two weeks before I had been in Jerusalem elbowing my way through the Arab bazaar toward the Church of the Resurrection, a Crusader construction, which obscured the starkness of Golgotha and the tomb. Devotional accretions laid a veneer on the central event of Christianity so that the original experience was mostly lost in the shadows, in the pounding sticks of the Turkish guards who ushered in the Orthodox priests, and in the noise of the milling crowds.

The past beckoned to the future. I glimpsed or halfway envisioned what would happen in my early days as a priest. Administration was new for me; but I liked organization and working with other people on a common problem. The boys at Jesuit High were an enthusiastic lot, a good challenge, but they were appreciative. I would need to get away from school to exercise some other priestly ministry—preaching and perhaps giving some retreats. My retreat last spring might be a springboard for helping others grope their way towards articulating their faith. The waves kept thundering in. A huge pine log was rolling back and forth in the sea, kicking up a wake as the tide pulled and tugged it. I laid down and drifted off. The future was never as real as the past, but it was more powerful. It lured me with its siren call. Its charm lifted me out of the fatigue and grind of work, of sculpting out my life from the contours of reality.

Three years went swiftly. In June, 1975, I was invited by Jim, the rector, to give two retreats in Hawaii. My first time to direct a retreat, I read several articles on the *Spiritual Exercises,* pumped Jim's experience about what to do and what to expect, and prayed fiercely to succeed. A rumpled heavy-set man given to sleeping through my homilies, Jim's gruffness shook some and charmed others. I was charmed and encouraged. In the exotic islands several Maryknoll sisters greeted us with leis. Bali Hai and the South Pacific and an enchanted island loomed before me. Swimming in the greenish blue sea was wonderfully relaxing, and each day I had a chance to stroll the beach and play in the surf, unwinding after three frenetic, often tense, years since ordination. Those three years as a priest passed swiftly through my memory as I flopped down on the soft sand and gazed back at myself on the other side of the horizon.

Boy, it was great unwinding on the beach, my chest heaving and my back scratching the sand. I did not feel the chest tension that I had for a couple of years. Every spring it came on like the pollen; I thought I had angina. The doctor prescribed relaxation. Rather impossible. I never had enough time to get it all done: teaching two classes of English, correcting papers, working out schedules, calming harassed teachers and then the marathon call at St. Cecilia's, saying two Masses, preaching at six and hearing confessions twice in between Masses. Where were those lovely roses now and the grand symphonic music that rang in my ears in the latter days of Rome?

School had finished, that first year, and I had made my annual retreat at the novitiate at Sheridan with Gordon, a director I admired very much, perhaps too much. As I revved up the car to make the ascent up the formidable Sheridan hills, I had high expectations of picking up from the previous year that rather glorious ordination retreat which had been so renewing in my commitment to community. After all those talks with Arvesu, some unknown missions, totally undefinable, beckoned my expectant spirits. The Sheridan novitiate's emptiness reminded me of Galloro, only there was some life stirring there. About 30 novices remained behind in the cavernous spaces built to house over 160 Jesuits—quite a contrast to my day when we filled the house with strained laughter.

My eagerness on this retreat tripped me up at every step. Dryness and desolation. What the hell did God want me to do; absolutely nothing came to me and I tasted the dust of the late summer. Abandoned, I rambled on about inconsequential ideas to Gordon, all of which was humiliating. My admiration for him precluded frankness, and only a blurred line led through this past year of frustrating achievement to the intensely exciting moments of the ordination retreat.

One evening I was walking through the spacious dining room overlooking the green valley and behind it Reservoir Hill, reaching up into the woods. In some hopefulness I flipped on a nameless symphony. I was puzzled and bewildered. The music recalled the retreat last year but evoked nothing more. I looked into the darkness outside the window into a mirror of my own interior darkness. No column of light lit the way. As I groped through my unresolved feelings of confusion, I cried. Years later Gordon said it had been one of the more unpleasant retreats to direct because he could not see what was happening. He said it was like looking through a darkened sunshield on a pane of glass. Something was going on in there, but he could not begin to make it out.

From hopefulness my days had passed to earnestness and persevering work. I could prove myself by hard work. The academic vice principal's job was tiring and the weekend work in the parishes was exhausting, but I felt good about being able to preach and hear confessions.

Jim, the rector, and Mike, the principal, were supportive so I felt good about my job. I had a wonderful house with all the pleasantries and accoutrements built on a pile of stilts. So long as I did not look down I could avoid the vertigo of failure.

Basking in the Hawaiian sands I was finally unwinding from these pent-up tensions. Maybe now I could get in touch with those joyous moments which had spurred me before. Flowing with the grace of the waves and sculpting a wake in the sultry blue, young bronzed Adonises were skating on the surf. I gazed out beyond them scanning the skies for some coastline.

Last summer four Jesuit scholastics and I had made retreat together on the Pacific beach. I thought this group retreat might enkindle the same spirit I had felt in our group ordination retreat. We had rolled up to a rambling, clapboard beach house in the Oregon Coast dunes. I walked steadily up the Oregon beach as the sun lifted the fog, the sea rocked and rolled with power and steam clung to the surface then wafted towards the lazy clouds. The beach was deserted except for squawking seagulls whose privacy I invaded. At the south end of the beach was a sandy estuary and across it a seaside town nestled against the mountain that plunged down into the swelling sea. The haze shielded the town from direct view. In the evening as the air cooled, the steam lifted and the sun shone brightly and clearly against the coast. The sharp mountain lines bristled with power and confronted the surging waves which battered their base. The town shook off its hazy mantle and the deserted beach awakened with clam diggers, beach jeeps and an occasional state patrol car.

In the evening after a hearty spaghetti dinner, we gathered around the porch in huge stuffed chairs to share our thoughts and prayers for the day. I had been reading Johannes Metz' *Poverty of Spirit,* the only highlight of the retreat. I said to our group: "Poverty is one's Christian vocation. The awareness that I am not worthy forces me to depend on Christ. But I can't do this simply out of need. Genuine love makes me poor." Ron said: "My riches are the things in which I find security." What he said reminded me of a line from Bonhoeffer: "Do not let us think that we can go it alone." So the retreat ended on a helpful, undefined note.

Later that summer a grim tragedy struck the province. It was St. Ignatius Day, July 31, 1974, when I heard the news. As I was going into the chapel to celebrate Mass, one of the brothers told me Peter, a scholastic, had been found dead in his room in Spokane. Later we drove from Portland to the beach for the feast day. One priest said: "I can't match the words with the reality." The Provincial had asked me to convey the message to Gordon, the novice master. When I met him he was at the beach at the point where the Nestucca River flows into the ocean. The wide blue expanse of the river was as still as a lagoon and a patch of fog sleepily drifted through the sky. The novices were stunned—only the calm pounding of the surf echoed in the wind as the wood smoke from the crab pot drifted up to meet the sun-drenched fog.

That day there was a mix of reports about Peter's history —about a possible heart attack, depression, and finally the grim news that he had hanged himself.

At the funeral in Spokane, Pat, his rector, said: "We are called to experience the joys of the resurrection as well as the doubt of his agony—to live his life with him, both the heights of the Transfiguration and the depths of trial and Temptation. Peter lived both."

The retreat in Hawaii with the Maryknoll sisters was going

well. They were new at this sharing experience and I was all ears. The less I said the less chance there was of making a mistake. Slowly I loosened up a bit more and started suggesting ways of praying or of overcoming blockages. These seemed to resonate with the sisters. The combination of drifting on the ocean waves with prayerful, rather intense conversation rocked me gently and I unwound.

I reflected on what it meant to have a deep life of prayer and how one came to know the Lord better in a retreat. I became aware, as a retreat director, how resistance to prayer occurred. We fight a rearguard action to maintain the *status quo.*

One of my own compulsive needs is for perfection. It is illustrated by my comment: "You do what you can and it's never enough," and my friend's response: "You do what you can and that's plenty!" Any acknowledgement of failure or sinfulness was difficult for me. Confessing failure and treating needs in spiritual direction was for me a depressing experience because it tampered with my drive for perfection.

Several years later I came to realize that the counterthrust to perfectionism is the mercy of God, the kindness of God. *Hesed* is the Hebrew word for tenderness, the kindness of love expressed by Hosea: "When Israel was a child I loved him . . . I was like someone who lifts an infant close against his cheek" (Hosea 11:1-4). Most basic disorders are connected with a lack of awareness of God's love. This mystery of love contains a presence beyond understanding.

After the first eight-day retreat was finished, Jim and I had four days before the next retreat so we arranged for a little junket around the island, which would include Molokai, the leper colony, on the way back. We flew in a small, cramped plane to the island of Hawaii and stayed at a Franciscan church in Hilo.

This was sugar cane country. The smell reminded me of the sickening sweet odor of cotton candy at a country fair. In the evening I reflected: "The bending sugar cane, sickening sweet as molasses, waving to the azure sea can, in time, become monotonous. Here the great dream finally pales under the harsh sun. At home on the Dakota plains one can sit in the shade of the billowing cottonwoods or even gaze on a snow-drifted plain and dream. In Hawaii, the Polynesian playland of enervated Americans grown slightly plump, the Bali Hai's of the South Pacific roll out with the rippling tide. No wonder the drug culture, violence and body cults thrive here. The world's blandishments are not enough; no rational system can put all the parts together.

"The church here is also dying. It was built in the 1920's, a monument to 17th century Franciscan Italian art. What can these trappings say to natives floundering in 20th century technological confusion? A place in the forest overlooking a volcano would make more sense. If we could close all the churches for 20 years, and begin from our human roots, we would all be much better off. If we built from God's creation, then we could say with Ireneus of Lyons 'the glory of God is man and woman, fully alive.' "

The next day we flew to the leper colony at Kalaupapa on Molokai where Fr. Damien had worked for 14 years with those afflicted with leprosy. The local priest greeted us quickly and then we dashed from house to house to bless the colonists. Those in their homes had mild forms of the disease: a lost hand, a disintegrating nose. At the hospital the deformities were worse. Toes and hands and part of the face were dissolved like stone with acid. Some had a hollow, throaty voice. The priest set a frenzied pace, without explanation, as if the blessings were an obligatory ritual for every visiting priest. *Poor devils must feel intruded on. A spectacle without rules. It's bad enough to be dumped here without the curious, well-meaning religious tramping through here.* I was ill-prepared for the physical deformities we encountered and was little versed in Hansen's disease. Gradually the priest explained that years ago the colonists had been dumped here by their friends and relatives. They were put off the boat in the sea and made to swim for the island. One older lady said that when she was discharged here at age 12, her first decision was whether or not she wanted to swim for the island or simply sink beneath the calming azure waves. The people lived what appeared to be a lonely life of outcasts with a social stigma. After our whirlwind tour of the island, I grasped that they had a quiet sense of dignity that they shared with each other.

The youngest settler was 35; most were much older. One of the ironies was that the State of Hawaii now wanted to move the lepers out of Kalaupapa to another hospital or settlement in order to develop a major resort at the beautiful beach peninsula.

When we left the island I was so anxious from my visit that I was without sleep for a night; the memory of the little town with shanty houses and government buildings haunted me. I could hear the ominous breeze wafting through the trees by the cemetery which lined the main road into the little town where Fr. Damien had labored to dig simple graves for the dead who were often left out in the open or buried in graves too shallow to be protected from the roving dogs.

I tossed and turned in a nightmarish recall not only of the past week but also of the past year and the turmoil that it had brought. When I had finished two years as the academic vice principal the year before, a shift of administration was in store. I had expected and hoped to be principal though I was young and inexperienced. Two lay teachers questioned how well they could deal with me; they found me aloof and at times enigmatic. A flurry of meetings had decided the question; I was appointed principal. The difficulties were resolved on the surface, but beneath the uneasy resolution lurked a few undetonated land mines.

My tensions as principal had mounted, but I did not always recognize them. In the spring when the pollen blew and the school year drew to a crescendo of activities and problems, my own responsibilities increased. Thus in April, which Eliot calls "the cruelest month," I again had bouts of chest tension and also hay fever, verging on asthma because of the tension. I had not had asthma for 18 years, since I was a kid. The doctor prescribed rest but gave no formula for it. In fact, the short spring vacation of a week compounded the tension because then I felt the dual need of getting away, but also of getting mounds of paperwork done. Nonetheless I managed and things went fairly smoothly.

When I became principal, I was much more independent. The previous principal, Mike, now the president, felt, with reason, that the principal should be left with freedom. Thus I had much more responsibility than I was accustomed to and at the same time more actual work. One thing I found in administration: it takes me time to make hard decisions and especially to unwind and distance myself from them afterwards.

As a vice principal, where I could lean on somebody else, I felt liked and needed. My mother once told me: "You've always been a good second in command." As a principal, I had to be more aggressive, stand out more and be responsible for both the achievements and the poor results of the school. The anxiety resulted in a waste of energies, a waste in not daring to do the work commensurate with my abilities.

I found later in psychotherapy that more independence played into a couple of weaknesses I had: the need for approval of those I admired, especially of authority figures; and, because of a weakness in self identity, I felt the need to be right and on top of things. I took failures in school, lack of order, conflicts with faculty as personal challenges or criticism.

At the time I recognized little of this conflict. I had strong reasons, I later found out, for repressing these conflicts. My psychosomatic chest tensions distressed me but I did not know what I could do about them.

Sometime prior to this I had read Karen Horney's comments about how the less self-conscious, the less intimidated a person is, the better he or she can express whatever gifts one has. At the time I certainly did not have this perspective nor this freedom. I regularly complied with the expectations of others.

I felt I should be able to handle any conflict, work or challenge that came along. Without admitting it, I could not. My concept of the apostolate was to do the *magis,* the Ignatian motto for the very best. For me this literally meant "more" work, and so my personal identity was tied up with working which was also the source of my Jesuit identity. Personal and Jesuit identity were practically the same, with "work" being the middle term.

On that nightmarish night in Hawaii, as I slept in fits and starts, several events from the year before stood out as traumatic. In the fall of my first year as principal, we had an uncommonly large number of student accidents. A freshman broke his arm on the football field. Another frosh was riding a bike and was hit by a car driven by one of the parents. After I sent off the student—largely uninjured—by ambulance to the hospital, I confronted the distraught driver. A junior, in climbing an electric pole was shocked, fell 30 feet, but somehow survived. Several other accidents occurred. Finally one day while I was teaching another Jesuit rushed into the room saying a student was dying in the school office. I ran into the office and a priest was anointing Tim with the oil of the sick. Tim had a congenital heart condition and had had a couple of operations for it. The doctors thought he was now fine. He had been playing touch football, was not feeling well, came to the office, and collapsed at the counter. By the time the paramedics arrived, he had turned blue. He briefly revived. I said something to him when he, in a daze, asked a question. But he died on the way to the hospital. The funeral was held at the school.

The end of the school year was stressful in a different way, and not nearly so dramatic or tragic. I was responsible for graduation. During the ceremonies the seniors were unusually rambunctious and raucous. Afterwards I was in the recreation room when several Jesuits started grousing about it. I became upset and stormed out of the room. I was frustrated and tired and I felt accused.

By the end of the school year, 1975, these conflicts were left unresolved and raging within me. I did not recognize their seriousness and felt greater efforts would solve any problems I was aware of. As I lay in bed the bitterness of some of these memories now surged within me triggered by the gruesome images at the deceptively idyllic Molokai. Physically sick, I retched, a taste like burnt coffee mixed with acid poured through my mouth and stung my nose. Finally I relaxed. An uneasy peace came over me, the motors quit churning within me and I fell into sleep.

Before long I was flying back to Oregon, aware that a huge chunk of nameless emotions had stirred within me, rather content that the retreats had gone so well and looking forward to my own retreat the following week. I thought now that after two rather dismal experiences at my own annual retreats I had the insights and confidence to make a retreat that would harken back to the ordination retreat at Galloro and the invigorating journey from Rome to Jerusalem.

The past three whirlwind years had propelled me through a maze of conflicts and satisfactions. I had not been able to sort them out clearly. My idealism in Jesuit life was still intact, but I had not come to grips with the insecurities of the people I worked with; I had many of my own that were buried.

Some of them emerged inchoately as I walked from the dunes down to the beach along the breaking water. The log was now fixed on the beach—a temporary permanency. I glanced back at my footprints in the wet sand. The foamy water had already washed most of them away and sandpipers pecked at my heels for flies. Ahead of me the sun darted in and out of the cloud cover blowing in with the waves and sea gulls floated and drifted, floated and drifted in soundless currents.

December, 1982

"Are you still working on your book?" It's Sunday, you should be relaxing." "This is relaxation, Tony. I'm dialoguing with Kuder, my literary therapist."

Molokai and Jerusalem were worlds apart. No, I didn't see the connection between the oriental invitation to life and the death sentence of the lepers. Do you sense there is one? Jerusalem beckoned to me a new world and a new creation. I thought Hawaii did too. They both deceived me with beauty, the lure of their charm. Loneliness and decay choked my tempestuous yearning for life. I did not see the lepers' dedication for each other then; compassion was not something I could see.

Under the usual gray-sky rain, Christmas trees, fat, full and fresh from the cutting, were strapped to the tops of a dozen different cars moving swiftly through the traffic. On the way to Seattle the Freemont Bridge was closed and traffic backed up for five miles when a large flatbed truck dumped several hundred trees smack in the middle of the freeway.

Woodland, Longview, Kalama, Trojan plant, the Cowlitz —the bus to Seattle is a good ride and quick. Gene Cobb's funeral, out there in the seaside coast yesterday was simple and moving. Jerry and Tony and I were all gathered together at the Coast last June for Gene's baptism. Jerry used ocean water. Was it out of a shell? Maybe. I don't remember. Water, death, and new life were intertwined.

Chapter Four
WAVES OF OBLIVION

Days One to Seven

I drove over from the high school to the "new" novitiate in Portland, a former convent school which resembled a small Bavarian castle, especially at night when the pale moonlight cast a bluish specter on the three-story edifice. Rested and relaxed, I entered into this retreat with zest. Bob, my director and good friend, was a patient, intuitive person with an almost naive assumption of everyone's goodness. Occasionally when he felt betrayed, his Irish temper blazed below the surface.

At the beginning of the retreat, Damien, the leper priest of Molokai, flashed through my mind. After 14 years in the leper colony, he died of leprosy at age 49. At 35 I was the same age as he when he had arrived at Kalaupapa and started building sewerage lines and water pipes, and digging graves. The Psalmist's refrain "you have chastened me, O Lord, but you have saved me from death" ran like a ribbon through my mind. Praying over the parable of the Sower and the Seed, I felt my ground was thorny, choked with obscure emotions that prevented growth and harvest. In a few days my emotional state picked up; in my dreams I felt carried away by charging horses and a few images of death came sweeping by. Asked to bury my fears, I was a man who had no strength, "like one forsaken among the dead" (Ps. 88:4-5).

As I was praying, an enigmatic phrase, like a signpost in an open meadow, flashed through my prayer, "Please don't eat the daisies." Now it was daisies instead of roses, but both were distractions from traveling towards the Lord on this inward journey. Passing fancies could sidetrack me. Fleeting consolations or self-indulgence with fantasies of past failures or daydreams were illusory.

These fears strained me but I unwound when I explained them to Bob, who was an eager, attentive listener, a gentle man.

Some dreams were particularly strong: an image of a bulbous red-robed cardinal with bulging dark eyes and thick glasses, riding on a Honda into Rome. Spiritual pride could warp and bloat the ego. The simplicity of Abraham, the father of faith, called to an unknown land, gave a mysterious promise of renewal. Daytime gave way to a less hazy sense of being with Jesus on a grassy meadow spangled with spring flowers. I was draped out on the hillside green listening to his gentle words. One night a golden haze clung to the forested, darkened hills of West Portland. To the south was Mount Tabor park, ringed in pinks and murky rose. The blazing yellow skies receded slowly into pale blue and then navy darkness.

Nighttime: my dreams gargled up a fearsome apocalyptic Angel of Death which swelled to a tidal wave. Suddenly the scene shifted to brilliant, tropical colors, surrounding the death struggles of baboons. Large behemoths bellowed and groaned in combat-royal. Suddenly my bedroom was filled with a horrible, buzzing sound and a terrible, ominous presence. Beelzebub, in the form of a large, furry, winged insect, was suffocating me. I woke with a start, flipped on the light, crept to the window and on the screen was a huge insect clinging to the webbing of the screen. I shooed it away, sighed in relief and went back to bed.

An emotional change came over me. The threat of an engulfing tidal wave thrilled me by its beauty and power. Out of the blue I asked: "Who are you?" "I am the Way, the Truth and the Life," came the response.

Strong contradictory feelings rose up within me: great joy, heart pumping and ready to go, but also strong sexual fantasies, bone-marrow tenseness. My old self strained at the abandonment. What was the "Way" all about?

In my confusion, I prayed the Mangificat of Mary:

My soul proclaims the greatness of the Lord
and my spirit exults in God my saviour;
because he has looked upon his lowly handmaid.

Luke 1:46-48

This prayer of praise became a prayer of acceptance. The tidal wave might smash me, but I would survive and be on the Way with the Lord. Anxiety, doubts and fears still surrounded me. A sense of the presence of the Lord, "I am with you," dispelled this desolation. In the early morning a voice came to me: "Get up! We are going to Jerusalem." Fear of the darkness and death came over me, then dissipated again. Some of the same peace I had felt from directing retreats in Hawaii coursed through my soul.

Responding to my images, Bob encouraged a relaxed pace and suggested a summary theme from the prophet Micah: "Act justly, love tenderly, and walk humbly with your God." Feelings and rebellion clashed with feelings of wanting to be with the Lord, even in the suffering of Calvary. I strolled around the landscaped gardens filled with pink and white petunias. Next to the chapel wall nestled a clump of hydrangea, still green, not pink or blue. The Lord still wanted to teach me something. In the garden I listened to the quiet around and within me. There was uncertainty and yet a peace that came amidst the doubt. A passage from Corinthians occurred to me: "There is a variety of gifts but always the same Spirit; there are all sorts of service to be done, but not all by you." Depend on others for your strength. In the still of the evening along the flowered path I heard: "Do you accept whatever is to happen?" Struggling through the neurotic defenses and rooted masquerades I said interiorly: "I do. Behold your servant." A word flashed through my mind: *sphragis*. Greek. But what did it mean? Sealed or signed? A kind of spiritual baptism that was engraved on the pliant fibers of the soul. A final surge of freedom was mingled with the phrase from Micah: "Walk humbly with your God."

Day Eight

By Sunday night I had finished the retreat. I was tired but happy and content after the emotionally charged eight days. I anticipated that more would eventually follow. In my happy tiredness, I recalled another refrain from long ago:

> In our rhythm of earthly life we tire of light.
> We are glad when the day ends, when the play ends;
> and ecstasy is too much pain.
>
> Chorus from the Rock

Just as I was starting to unwind, ever so little, I felt driven to the chapel to pray, pushed on by a deep and urgent call to respond once more to the Lord. I went to kneel in the chapel, gazed on the crucifix, and prayed to the Lord. Suddenly I was powerfully overwhelmed by feelings of love for the Lord. I felt I could live and die with and for him because of his great love for me. Then I got dizzy and I all but passed out in the pew. I felt I was going to die, bound by helpless rapture. Shaken and trembling, I groped my way breathlessly out of the chapel. I recalled the rapturous, ecstatic, almost erotic statue of Teresa of Avilla pierced by an angel's sword. It was a statue sculpted by Bernini and rested in a small church near Santa Susanna in Rome. How was this happening? More deeply I feared that it could happen again.

I wandered around the novitiate grounds to calm down. I thought of talking to Bob, my director, but I was uncertain where he was and I was too embarrassed to talk about it. From that time on, I was never fully calm nor completely rational again. The tidal wave was looming on the horizon and my emotions were churning up inside me.

That night I could not sleep because I was so agitated and in such great emotional turmoil. Strong and passionate urges were wrestling for control. Finally about 2:30 in the morning I got up, went to the chapel, fearful that something powerful might happen again. But I had no place to turn for guidance, except to the Lord himself. I prayed over Galatians:

> What the Spirit brings is very different: love, joy,
> peace, patience, kindness, goodness, trustfulness, gentleness
> and self-control. There can be no law against things like
> that, of course. You cannot belong to Christ Jesus unless
> you crucify all self-indulgent passions and desires.
>
> (5:22-23)

Each word sank into my depths. Love, joy, and self-control were especially strong sentiments. I got the notion that somehow St. Paul had mixed up the order. Joy was not the second gift, but the last and most significant gift and the culmination of all gifts. At the end I felt calmer, though still agitated. I slept fitfully.

Day Nine

In the morning I was going through an interior crucifixion. I took down a crucifix from the wall and embraced it hoping for some relief. Finally a kind of Edenic peace flowed through me, and I imagined a gardener coming towards me with a gesture of peace. I sobbed with relief and still shaken I went to Mass and breakfast.

I talked in vague terms to Bob about my continuing prayer experience. He could see I was shaken and suggested I spend a day of rest before going back to the high school to start work. We did some shopping together, went to the bank and ran some errands. I was distracted and had a hard time concentrating and keeping in touch with Bob.

That Monday afternoon I visited at Jesuit High with three

or four other Jesuits. I was restless and have no remembrance of what was said. I made plans to get together with Bob again on Thursday.

After dinner the tension increased. Restlessly I went to the high school chapel to pray and then to my own room. A strange lightness filled me and a vision of the Court of Heaven with Bachian organ music came to me. As I pictured the scene, the Lord ascended to meet the Father. IHS (Jesus) was inscribed across the skies. Then a powerful aroma of lilies wafted across the room. This perfume both confused and thrilled me. I left my room and walked to the other end of the hall. Then I smelled analgesic balm which, it turned out, was the case. One of the Jesuits had bruised his leg, but I still clung to the smell of a room full of lilies. Perhaps in this altered state the senses, especially smelling, went awry and induced the scent of flowers. Confused I needed to see Bob immediately. So I set out to the novitiate across the city. I am not certain what I told him that night.

Day Ten

My foundations were shaky; I did not know what to expect. I went back to work in the principal's office. I did a number of ordinary office jobs, wandered around the campus, and planned for the new year. The day was a passing lull.

In my altered condition I was becoming much more aware of bodily sensations such as smells or a sneeze or a cough. In fact, around this time, I started to associate a sneeze caused by tension with a demonic spirit or with an obstacle to the Lord's will for me. Furthermore, I could look at flowers or people or the clouds and in their living light I detected a spirit breathing power and energy through them.

I could hardly sleep and I was spending long hours in prayer. Tuesday night I experimented with a few yoga positions for prayer. I did not know what I was doing, but it seemed that body movements and position either helped or hindered prayer. When I had been in Turkey in 1972, I had bought a deep blue, Moslem prayer rug which I had hanging on the wall. I took this down and started to pray on it— Moslem fashion. I felt that I was going through a strange, condensed version of the 30-day *Spiritual Exercises.*

Day Eleven

I could not concentrate on what I was doing in the office though I was making some feeble attempts to plan for the next year.

That afternoon I went out to the high school villa along the Willamette River with Bob. I think this was at his suggestion so that we could both relax. He tried to interest me in a White Sox game, but I could not concentrate. Then Arnie, a Jesuit parish priest, arrived. He had just returned from the Superiors' Retreat in Spokane where they had focused on how to assimilate the 32nd General Congregation, a Jesuit renewal meeting recently finished in Rome. I thought perhaps my own prayer experience would have something to do with this important Jesuit event. He made some joke in Spanish about an old fart, which I tried to understand.

Since I was exhausted, I took a nap, but pitched and turned and was highly agitated. Bob and I drove back in to town, and I discussed the need for renewing and helping women religious who were so cramped by their life style, prayer life and traditional habits.

I had dinner that night with Bill, a newly ordained Jesuit who was a chaplain at the hospital. I drifted through the conversation. I recall talking about compassion, intuiting how people feel, and the healing which occurs through caring. I said I was becoming more and more aware of how a healthy mind makes for a healthy body.

That night I was more restless than ever. I slept on the floor because it seemed more comfortable. In my imagination, I pitched my tent on the hills of Galilee. "The birds of the air have nests, foxes have holes, but the Son of Man has nowhere to lie his head." Sometime in the night a waking dream came to me of the Two Standards in the *Spiritual Exercises* which pits the standard of Christ against the standard of Satan. On one hillside was Christ with a band of followers. Across the valley was Satan, the old Fart, pumping swamp gas. I joined up with Christ and his followers although I did not see him, and only talked to his followers. They all called me "the rookie." After a time I asked someone what my job would be. He said: "You're a rookie for a long time." Then I went to the end of the line and someone with a book wrote down my job: I was to be a "scribe" and sometime later I would be a "discerner." I wondered where we were all going. I had been sealed *(sphragis)* with the Lord and I was inscribed with *Insignis,* a Latin word, which for Jesuits means to be outstanding in some way.

Day Twelve

The next morning I took a shower and halfway believed I was swimming in the cold waters of the Sea of Galilee. After drifting through the day trying "to discern" where I was going, I had dinner with Joe who had just returned from Israel, which fired up my imagination with all the sights of Galilee. Then I said I thought the years after Vatican II would have the same outpouring of the Spirit, the same influx of divine power into the church and the same direct experience of God which the saints had after the Council of Trent. These years after Vatican II would be recounted by historians with the same enthusiasm as the accounts of the Counter Reformation after Trent.

I kept praying for Bob because I felt he was going through the same experiences which I was. I also spent several hours composing and writing out some prayers. My lengthy prayer that night centered on 1 Corinthians and the gift of discernment. I was trying to figure out what being a "discerner" meant. The text of 1 Corinthians 12:14 vibrated with life and each word pulsated with a deeper meaning for me. I had a genuine sense of discerning the Lord's gifts.

Then I experienced a sensation of being physically implanted with the vows of poverty, chastity and obedience, as if this were a deeper significance of the *sphragis.* They became wholly a part of me. Deeper yet was an intuition that I was to live these out with Christ in poverty, humiliation and in cold. I then took another shower in Lake Genneserat; I was terribly cold. I felt a chill for several hours and shivered and trembled. Back in my room I passed out and came to shortly afterwards. Origen, the Alexandrian theologian, was right: reincarnation was a fact. As I went to close my curtains, I noticed the moon was almost full.

Day Thirteen

I slept briefly that night. When I awoke I was immensely afraid of going blind from the light. Besides that, everything I saw or heard reminded me of a gospel parable.

Two Jamestown, North Dakota, farmers came into our dining room and one recounted how as a boy he had stayed out too late one night. Two hours later he was out plowing a field, having been ordered out to the field by his dad. He rigged up the plow so that at the end of a furrow a jerk of the plow woke him up. However, at the end of one furrow he slept on and the plow continued straight on through a field of 40 acres of oats. I made a kind of parable out of this story with the nonsense conclusion of "Don't sow your oats too late at night, lest you plow them under in the morning."

Then I felt an urgent need to warn Bob about the danger of suicide coming from the despair of reincarnation. Images of Peter's suicide flashed through my mind, so I raced back over to the novitiate, but could not find Bob. I was driving a VW stick shift and almost collided with another car. I somehow got back to school, talked with Dave, an old friend, now teaching in Missoula. To his bewilderment, I told him the oats parable. While I was talking to Dave, Jim called from the Provincial's office about lining up a meeting in October. I kept dancing around his questions saying I would not be able to plan anything for a couple of weeks. Somehow the whole next week and beyond would be blacked out so planning was useless. In fact, the president of the school, Mike, and I were going to get away for a break to the beach the following Wednesday, but I knew that was going to be impossible because of the coming darkness.

Then Dave and I went to lunch which I had planned as a celebration with wine and cheese and sandwiches for all those working at the school, including the students. I went around serving everyone like I was at Cana celebrating a party. Someone later said I seemed terribly tense. Little wonder.

After lunch I was living through one of the Gospels and was then called to the desert through temptations. I was afraid of succumbing to a Messianic temptation, the tremendous burden of saving others. A blinding light also flashed through my head, and I was fearful that I would be given a horribly draining power of healing the sick.

I broke down crying with Kevin, a Jesuit in the community, who said something like: "You don't have to do it all by yourself," and "You don't realize what a good person you are." Instead of going to Mass which I did not think I could get through because of its rich symbolism and my urgency to see the Lord in all things, I asked for Kevin's blessing and left the chapel.

I went to my room for some time, toyed with some writing and pondered what was going on. Every time I made a mistake writing it was a sign of a demonic force or lack of genuine discernment and I had to start over. This confusion occurred so frequently that I soon gave up. The tension was increasing so rapidly that I felt enormous pain all over my body. I felt as if my heart were pierced and my back nailed to a cross. Panicky, I sought out Bob's help. He calmed me down and I sighed with relief. We took a walk around the football field, sat for a while in the stands and I felt better though exhausted.

About then Jim, the rector, returned from giving retreats and I felt immense confidence that since he was in charge he would know what to do and I motioned Bob to talk to him.

That evening Kevin got me to stain some new shelving. It was a good effort to try to get my mind off what was going on, but it was far too late. My mind was feasting on Brueghelian images, demonic and angelic scenes and a riot of ideas. While I was staining the shelves, an interior voice called me to deepen my discernment. Each finger of my hand was a symbol of God's communication, and I imagined myself in Rome being the principal discerner at some council. I could not see anything, but someone would relay the information for me to discern on while I sat in an enclosure behind a black screen. My friend, Steve, was there to take care of me. This whole day was a living out of a dream sequence, like a sleep walk.

I then went back to my room and saw a vision of a hierarchy of dyings and risings of death and resurrection—the more death, the higher the position in the next life. It was horrifying. My mind was racing back and forth between visions of perfect harmony and nightmares of malevolent forces. Sometime then I died and came back to life and then I remembered I must have been killed in an accident in the VW that morning.

About then my folks actually called from Minnesota and asked if I could not come home a week later because of a conflict with a wedding. I had great joy at the call because I realized then they were in heaven with me and in a short time we would all be together.

Then I must have passed out because when I came to I felt a great need to see someone to tell them what was going on. I went down the hall to see Jim, the rector, with some line about the foolishness of the cross, dying with Christ, and being sent to Rome. He put his big mitts on my shoulders and told me to go to bed and to get some sleep, which I did for about the first time all week.

Day Fourteen

I woke up feeling better. But then immediately every object became a symbol of some aspect of God's love or some numinous insight. Kevin saw I was still intensely agitated so he took me on a "trust walk" with him. During the walk I had an image of an enormous distance of hierarchies of people in the church. I had to pass through them all, and I was at the beginning. The whole living church was praying for me so that I would make it through this crisis. I experienced more of the previous leaping, exultant ecstasy. Everything around me quivered with a life from beyond. Yet I dreaded its blinding force and the threats and honors which hovered behind it all. Elation carried me away in the violent wind of a jet stream.

I was fairly peaceful as long as I was walking with Kevin, but I came back into the kitchen and was "blinded" by an interior light. Then Jim was getting me ready to go to the hospital. A visiting Jesuit psychologist who happened to be there told Jim I was going through a psychotic episode and not to mess with amateurs. So we packed a few clothes and Jim and Bob took me to Providence Hospital. I was wearing a silly white shirt and black trousers. Jim was not the greatest connoisseur of clothes.

We arrived at the hospital and I was taken up to the psych ward on the 6th floor. I was tested relentlessly. A nurse or doctor asked me: "How many brothers and sisters do you have?"

"Eight."

"Is there any history of mental illness in your family?"

"I had a great aunt who was senile and a cousin who committed suicide."

"What have you been doing this past week?" "Have you been drinking very much?" "Have you been masturbating?" "Why do you think that you are in the hospital?" They asked me a couple of riddles and I had to explain what they meant: "What does this mean?" 'A rolling stone gathers no moss' and 'People who live in glass houses shouldn't throw stones?' "

A nurse took my temperature. I tried to control it, but could not. It rolled up to 102 degrees. A doctor with a steel mallet tapped all my extremities and reflexes for reactions. I flunked all the tests. I knew I would not be going to Rome for several years.

Someone gave me a shot. I climbed into bed in a sealed off room. It had a metal netting on the window. A TV monitor looked down on the bed from a corner in the ceiling. I was utterly exhausted. I had failed everything. I heard a silent, ominous roar coming closer and closer. Then mountainous waves surged in over me. I no longer fought it, but rolled, drifted and floated with the powerful current that swept me away from all moorings, from all previous security. A huge pine log floated on by me. Then I realized I had been pitching and rolling in the turbulent waves for a long, long time. And finally a blissful darkness and thankful peace came as I slipped off into the waves.

December, 1982

   There's a typewriter downstairs next to the boiler room or the laundry, the bowels of the building. Construction dust clung to the carpet, walls and junk-piled desk. Above, the carpenters pounded and hammered at the old walls. Looks like a street in Dresden, after the bombing.

   The new infirmary at Seattle University would be ready in March. Looks like there are several candidates already: McIntyre laid low by emphysema. O'Grady crippled by arthritis, Bussy with a host of ailments and McGoldrick, living on sheer will power at 88. Age is just a matter of mind. If you don't mind, it doesn't matter. That's what Harry says.

   Steve said his thesis has been like a snowball launched downhill for five weeks, gathering momentum and weight as it went. This week he needs to push the massive ball uphill, so it's a strain, especially before Christmas.

Chapter Five
THE HOSPITAL

Day 16

Came to, washed ashore, groggy, bedraggled, a sailor's binge. What day was it? Vaguely remembered having awakened a few times and taking some pills. Where did that TV monitor register? Got up and stared blankly at the glassed-in nurses' station where they dispensed the drugs. Were they talking to me? Something about breakfast. Shuffled on down to the day room and gazed inside. Slowly. Someone was with me.

Fifteen patients. Most were having breakfast at the far end of the long room. A pool table in the center. Next to the wall was a TV with chairs round it. Wandered down to the breakfast end. All were strangers, and out of place. Some people in jackets had tags on them. A therapist. One of them pulled out a tray with Howell on it from the rack. A standard menu of wet scrambled eggs, two steamed strips of bacon, a tasteless roll and orange juice. *Caffelatte e marmalade, per favore. Si, lo voglio. Oh, get it straight. My pronunciation was awful.* Orange juice came in plastic cups and pull-back paper lids. *Why did they have this kitchen in the middle of the hospital? Gosh, they looked droopy.* Plastic cups were common at pill time. A pill and a shot of apple juice.

Ate breakfast and looked around. Patients talking about the food. Someone filled out a menu. *Vorrei un cappucino e un dolce.* So who's sick? Wandered around the hallways and day room in pajamas and bathrobe. How were you supposed to dress? Everyone wore street clothes even when they were sick.

Dreaded having to tell anyone what had happened, especially parents. Shocked to be here and knew they would be shocked. *Just like poor Aunt Elfie. They took her off to Jamestown. "My nephew will take care of me. I know Joe will take care of me."* Patients and therapists were distant. Why did they keep smiling?

The day room became the center of our activities. Some of us formed the coffee clutch, the adolescents shot pool and some watched TV regularly at night. Shortly got to know two women patients rather well. Seemed the sanest and friendliest of the group. Betty, about 33, married with a couple of kids. Had taken an overdose, I heard, but caught it in time. People played for keeps here. *Why do people do such crazy things? Keith's girlfriend tried to do that a couple of times, but she never seemed that serious about it.* A religious sister, about 50, was the other woman. Very depressed and carried the world's burdens on her slightly stooped shoulders. Wore gray clothes. Had a quiet friendliness. *Didn't know that nuns ended up here too. Couldn't think of any nuns who had gone off their rocker. My fourth grade teacher was a candidate.*

All these sights only gradually came into focus for me. The first three days I was in a daze and not much registered. Several compulsive features of the "retreat" week remained with me. *Trust. I had to trust. I had to trust the doctors and nurses. Flashed in my head like a neon commercial. Trust. Trust. What else? If I could only remember then I could be well again. Where did those locked doors go to? Everyone had keys around this place. I'll get my razor blades at the nurses' station. I don't know why they don't trust me. I'm not going to do anything. Maybe it's the other patients. There are some real whackos here.*

About three doctors were in charge of me. Dr. Colbach was in overall charge. He was intense and solicitous and urgently professional. Later in the year he was quoted in Portland's newspaper, *The Oregonian,* in an article on psychiatry and mental patients. *I wonder if they ever got all that sewage at Crater Lake cleaned up last week.* After I had been in the hospital two weeks Colbach invited me to join him in talking to a group of 25 police officers. We got in the doctor's car. He was kind of quiet. "This group meets with me once a week for a course I'm giving them on dealing with mental patients, especially those they find out on the streets. You were rather fortunate that your friends brought you into the hospital." The policemen were eager to look like they knew their job. They asked me a number of questions, but at the coffee break they left me alone. They hadn't learned their lesson very well.

Another psychiatrist, Dr. Zieverink, also started seeing me during my hospitalization since he was going to treat me after I left the hospital. He wore glasses. He had a beard that was almost neat. Where was his skull cap? He asked me a few questions about how I was doing in the hospital. He seemed competent.

Another doctor was a neurosurgeon and had a thousand questions about my medical history. I spent a couple of days going through tests and X-rays. A memorable day was spent with a brain scanner in which I was flipped into about eight different prone positions for shots of my brain. "I do this about twice a day. Now hold it. That's it. Nice and easy. These things blur easily." All physical and chemical aspects of the body seemed to check out normal, at least I was not told otherwise. I had felt in the later stages of the psychotic episode that my body chemistry was changing. Even my sweat smelled different.

One of the patients. A guy. Came back from electric shock treatment today. They had some fancy name for it. Never could remember it. Betty said: "I think he's squared around finally. He sure looks shot though."

Bill added: "It takes about a day for them to come out of it."

The two psychiatrists stopped by about every other day, except weekends, to check on medications and how I was feeling. I was taking 400 mg. of Thorazine, an anti-psychotic.

We spent a lot of time talking about side effects and what the Thorazine was supposed to do. I had an innate skepticism of drugs so my resistance level was high to any medication.

I could hear my dad saying, "I had five customers today who were all taking too much medicine. Those doctors get sick of seeing them and prescribe drugs to keep them busy. I fill more tranquilizers in a day than I used to in a month. They're hooked."

One of the patients was a druggist who had been mugged. About 70, he had several cuts and wounds on his balding head. He had amnesia and could not remember his wife. She was frequently there, weeping softly, trying to be cheerful. I tried to cheer him up, but he could not get beyond the drugstore. "Henry, how's the drugstore today? Rexall isn't it? My dad had a Rexall drugstore too. We used to have Rexall products all over the house. Superplenamins, vitamins. Yep, I know you sold a lot of them. So did my dad."

The average length of stay in the hospital was 21 days. I stayed longer so had a chance to see the comings and goings of many patients. "You came in on a full moon. The ward is always full when the moon's out. Then it tapers off again." One fellow was a recovered alcoholic. He had recently gone off the wagon after ten years of sobriety. Since he himself was an alcohol counselor, he did not want to go through the normal alcohol treatment centers so he had found an anonymous mental health ward.

"Pat," he said, "have you ever read *Macbeth?* 'All our yesterdays have lighted fools the way to dusty death.' That's what it's all about."

I added: "It is a tale told by an idiot, full of sound and fury, signifying nothing. Good poetry, but too bleak for me."

I asked one of the therapists: "Have you ever thought of reading novels to some of the patients? One of my English teachers at Gonzaga University used to read *Wuthering*

Heights to mental patients with good success. They could identify with the mood and it helped them to express their emotions.''

"I'll have to look into that. Sounds like a good idea, Pat.''

Betty was the only other hard-core coffee drinker, so we spent a lot of time together over coffee, dryly observing the patients in the day room, talking about the staff and the unit. Neither of us touched on the past. We knew better or probably did not even think about it, but naturally drifted into safe subjects.

The first week I was deluged with visitors, especially priests. The last thing I wanted was visitors, especially helpful priests.

"How are you feeling?''

"Oh, fine.''

"Anything I can get you?''

"No, I've got everything I need.''

Act normal. They think you're crazy. Put on a good front. They're going to be talking to everyone in the city. As patients, we were more comfortable among ourselves when we could joke about "going bananas.'' It was no joke talking about the "crazies'' with real people. They were too concerned. I also noticed that many of the other patients were hyper and agitated when their families visited them or when they went out on a "home visit.'' These were often mixed blessings.

One heavy-set Providence sister would amble through the ward on a visit and was a pleasant addition. She always talked about innocuous subjects. The past was painful and the future was too doubtful.

I've got to get out of here by St. Ignatius Day—July 31. That will wrap up the whole retreat. Then I'll know it was all real. When I questioned the doctors about a release time, they always responded vaguely. Progress was a daily thing and they had no apparent schedule. I would go home when I was "well'' or "all better.''

By my request, no visitors, except my rector, Jim, saw me after the first week. The daily order was very routine; we looked forward to meal time, to recreation and to seeing the doctor. The hospital regime was similar to the novitiate at Sheridan in its grimmer aspects.

Fourteen years ago. I rode up that long hill at Sheridan in a Trappist truck. Crazy, huh? Tom and I stayed at the Trappist monastery the night before to prepare ourselves for entering the Jesuit novitiate. It was supposed to be a day of prayer at the monastery, but bulldozers roared up and down the hill to lay a new pipeline. A second-year Jesuit novice said: "We have ice cream on Thursdays and villa days. That's Tuesdays." Every minute was clocked from rising at 5 to retiring at 9:37. Daily order hardly ever shifted. Just like this ward. One day flows into the next. At the end of the hall there's a sign: "Today is Saturday. July 26." Novitiate play-orders gave some relief. I liked handball and was good at it, even on those slick, wet days that we always got in the winter. It was a time of peace. Prayer. Work and play. With a little Latin thrown in from Fr. Mullen. "Try translating that as 'a lion's share.'" He spruced up our translations with crispness that came from being a high-school principal in three schools.

In the psych ward, we began the day after breakfast by doing our chores and then by having a group meeting of the patients for communal decision making. One of us was elected president and we volunteered for various jobs around the ward, such as taking the towels out of the showers. *I wonder if she is in there now. I wouldn't want to pop in there while she's naked. On the other hand. Just like the time I pulled back the shower curtain and someone jumped out.* This volunteering involved a lot of tugging and pulling. There was an expectation by the staff, and gradually by the group members, that everyone would do something. Their chores were minimal, but new patients often resisted any responsibility whatever.

Most of the meetings were spent on three topics: assignment of chores, field trip possibilities, talking about petty annoyances, such as no one answering the phone or a radio on too late or too loud. These meetings served the added mixed blessing of having individuals express to a large group how they felt about something.

The morning-shift staff ran these meetings, usually an older nurse in her 50's, who had arthritis in her hands and was often wringing her hands to exercise them. She sometimes appeared less relaxed than the patients. Most of the staff were younger, in their mid-20's. The young ones had finished their training recently and were enthusiastic and attractive people. They were pleased when we got up enough energy to go on a field trip to a rose garden or to a park for a picnic. Only the patients who were halfway recovered from the shock of their breakdown went on a picnic. The first three or four ward days were "zombie" days. The patients were still in a daze or sometimes totally exhausted from internal punishment or were often recovering from self-inflicted physical wounds.

One nurse stood out from the rest. Lillian, a somewhat shriveled lady of 55. With a thoughtful, shrewd glance of her piercing eyes, she had a patient all sized up. When my humor returned, I called her the "Grinch," because of her looks. What we liked about her was that she admitted she was neurotic too. She just happened to be a healthy neurotic at the moment. We were curious about her, but never bold enough to ask the types of questions she asked us. Our coffee klatch liked her; the real psychos were afraid of her and retreated from her gaze. Lillian was kind and encouraging though—you just felt that she had been through it all before you, so she knew what she was talking about. She had a devotion to the Little Flower, St. Therese, which intrigued me. She would not talk about it. She did say Therese was a neurotic; in fact, she claimed most of the holy people of the church were neurotics who worked through their sickness, were sometimes healed, and became saints.

She would work only four days a week because she got too wound up in what she was doing. Once she walked onto the ward and said: "This place is so tight I can feel it in my bones." Another time she said: "Every male thinks about sex every seven seconds. That's a heck of a lot of tension." *My engines weren't firing that often. Must be awfully distracting. Maybe that's why I'm so tense.*

My ideas were still jumbled; my idea of God was still magical and of my own making. I heard a homily once: "Let God be God. Let Him Love with all his being and be free." *If he's free, then I'm free. I was praying to the Father in Light inaccessible. That was the blindness part. I tried to enter into that laser light. I was rash and foolish. I lost sight of the Truth and met a punitive, petulant god of my own making.*

I was still depending on formulae to carry me through this recovery. My feelings were bruised. I could not talk to anyone about what had really happened. I was confused about my prayer experience, and I could not understand why I had a breakdown. I perceived no logical connection since I had been feeling great. I had had a good school year. I gave retreats in Hawaii, and was making a good retreat myself. I wondered if it was all that trauma at the leper colony. I was kind of upset that next night in Oahu when all those accidents flashed through my head. The doctors didn't have any explanation. They said it sounded like I was drinking a lot when I came to the hospital. I must have sounded more confused than I was. I said I drank a little wine for supper like St. Paul recommends. The Lord is healing my feelings and imagination and memories. All this gurgled up from my psyche. Out of control. The retreat put me in touch with a lot of powerful feelings. I didn't know their names. Maybe that was the point of the whole retreat.

At the end of my first week in the hospital, two Jesuit

friends, Don and Steve, called. I said I had "Hathaway's disease." Secretary of the Interior Hathaway from Wyoming had just resigned from the cabinet because of nervous exhaustion. I said no more because I had to keep up a good front. I dreaded having to face others when I got out of the sheltered cocoon of the hospital. Here I could continue the facade of being all right and close myself off from curious looks. After a couple of weeks in the hospital I could go outside for walks or shopping or occasional short visits home. I spent hours pacing the neighborhood. I knew every cranny and barking dog in the area. It was a well-kept residential area, and I enjoyed looking at the manicured lawns, the rose beds, hydrangea, daisies, marigolds, petunias, and a profusion of shrubs and hedges. *"Pat, you were always bringing home flowers to me from the neighbors—roots and all." I thought Mom liked flowers. They weren't doing any good there by the garage.* I felt at times I was coming to life and seeing it all for the first time. I was never very tired as I had been at times before, but I was extremely restless and I could not sit still long enough to read, write or even to watch TV. One show I watched upset me a great deal. Because of its violence, it triggered memories of the chaos of my breakdown.

I would project what I would do next week and then tear it all up. It was impossible to plan beyond a couple days because planning depended so directly on the way I felt. *Right now glass was churning up in my stomach. A long ache ran from my neck to my hips like I had been typing for twelve hours straight.*

All these impressions are more relativized and placed in perspective than my own thoughts were at the time. For the most part, I was confused about what had happened, fearful about the future and mortified that I was sick. I tried to keep a bit of a journal, which was a sporadic project. Here are some entries:

Day 29 - 14th day of the hospital:

Towards evening I had a severe headache in the front left lobe. Some of the tension from my gut and chest had passed to my head. The tension early in the day was like that of asthma, except I did not have the wheezing phlegm.

Day 30:

I went jogging and played croquet. For the first time my thoughts are not racing on ahead. The physical fatigue from exercising enables me to concentrate on the simple functions of staying alive. My brother Mike, who is a doctor, called so I told him what I have—an acute psychotic reaction. After delaying for a week, I had called my folks to tell them I had had a breakdown. I did not want to face them because I felt guilty. I knew when Mike called that they had all talked it over. Mike was the expert since he was a doctor, so he had to probe what was really going on. He did not find out much.

Day 31:

Everyone here has encouraged me by saying this illness will, in the long run, make me a better person, better integrated and more in tune with my own feelings. Earlier I had come to see that after the ninth day of the retreat, I was involved in a fair amount of delusion—especially about the capacity I had for handling what was happening.

There is a saying that a neurotic builds castles in his mind, but that a psychotic moves into them. I believe that it was shortly after the ninth day that I started to move into my dreams. The reality they had was symbolic, possibly for the future. Signs are guidelines, but they are not an end in themselves.

Bob stopped by to see how I was doing.

Bob really understood what it was all about. If he would just explain what was going on with me to the doctors, then maybe I could get out of here. Spiritual health needs trust and working through appropriate authority.

I was bewildered and remotely angered by my relationship, or lack of it, to God. *Another blind spot is my image of God. Mystery. Light inaccessible. All powerful. Faust tried to touch or contain it too.*

Day 32 - The Feast of the Transfiguration:

The theme of my day seems to be that I need to be flexible enough in planning my day and my life to allow change and joy through my life. Some Jesuits can buttress their lives so that the bulwark of their inner core is untouched by either change or exuberance.

Day 33

I relied on retreat experiences for coherence and depth. *A person needs to listen, which involves faith, and to trust, which is hope. Allow mystery rather than puzzlement and magic. Openness is the opposite of rigid programming. Allow surprise. Old Testament: surprised in a different way by his 40 days of rain and Noah in his ridiculous ark. Allow joy. That's the end result of listening, trusting and relaxing. Ultimate wisdom.*

Jack, a diocesan priest, saw me tonight and mentioned that the president of Central Catholic High School had talked to all the priests about slowing down after what happened to me. *That's great. Now I'm an example for everyone in the city. Maybe God works through weak instruments. Jack could slow down himself.*

I went back to Jesuit High for a visit today. The academic vice principal, Jim, will be staying on through December as acting principal. *By then I'll be back in the saddle if I ever get released from this hospital. It all seems so long, so very long.*

Day 34:

I saw two doctors today. They have set next Wednesday,

August 13 as the probable release day. I was upset when Dr. Zieverink said that I could not resume the full duties as principal until January. After some discussion he modified that a bit and said that I could not go back until all parties concerned agreed that I could undertake the load again.

Much of what has happened in the last month reminds me of a 30-day retreat, though the time spent will actually be 40 days and 40 nights.

What is sainthood? Perhaps some journey will give meaning to this devastation.

Day 35:

Zieverink emphasized that these weeks "were to be devoted to Pat Howell." I wrote: "I am to attend to my own health above all else. I will need constant reminding of this." "Shoulds" and "duty" were a strong and pervasive force throughout my time in the hospital. I was dependent on authority to give me direction and reassurance. If sheer will power could have cured me, I would have been the healthiest man in town.

Mother's letter of August 4 arrived today: "The only news that I want to hear is that you are steadily improving. I have read that sometimes what has happened to you is the very best thing that can happen to a person. Your whole life still changes for the better. I am sure that you will learn to cope with all the stresses and strains of executive-type work. You are in my prayers many times during the day and night. God must have designed something special for you and I know that you will be ready to accept His challenge."

I was grateful for the letter, but it was also depressing. I hated the fact that I had to get well. I did not feel "special" at all. I felt like shit, réfuse to be thrown away.

Today my brother Bill arrived from Prosser, Washington, and we visited the rose gardens which were in full and glorious bloom. We got to sniffing the distinctive aromatic flavors.

Bill said, in his wonderful simplicity: "The rose garden

would be a beautiful place to bring a blind person." I took myself to be that person. In fact during these days I had a strong fear of going blind, probably triggered by seeing a blind woman, about 35 years old, who came to Mass each morning at the hospital. The previous night we had viewed a story about a man in his twenties who was blinded in a basketball game. He continued to run cross country and did several other energetic athletic activities. Finally I recalled the overwhelming blinding light that Moses experienced and the blinding light from the Lord on Mount Tabor.

Bill and I had a good six-hour visit, especially later in the Japanese Gardens: the iconic beauty of each shrub and setting soothed me. It was great to be with Bill.

The garden visit with Bill recalled the long, patient hours at the novitiate that I had spent planting azaleas, rhododendrons and numerous flowers. I loved the molding smell of leaves and the sharp maple intermingled with the pitch of the Douglas fir. We novices would meander through the sawdust strewn path.

At the novitiate I relished the solitude in the midst of new friends. When I entered I was at peace with myself. On the first long hike I was panting up the long Reservoir Hill in the back of the novitiate. I was young and in fairly good shape, I thought. In fact, I was a noodle physically when it came to hiking or handball. The second-year men were seasoned hikers, and I thought that first day at the novitiate we were headed out for a stroll. I had changed to some old clothes and my first pair of hiking boots. Rod, Randy and I sped on by the crisp ripening apple trees lining the drive and then raced up the hill. The grass was brown and the soil dry with cracks. My lungs were bursting when we reached the top. We scrambled over a stile. "Watch out for the poison oak." A bright red, russet orange vine curled around the stile. "Someone cut those for the chapel and wound up with a first class

case of 'oak,' swollen and bloated like a balloon."
A half hour later we rested briefly at "Stanhopes," an
abandoned farmyard. A tangle of blackberry vines covered a
collapsing barn and unkept apple trees and gnarled oak trees
sheltered the small, shuttered house. Nestled at the top of the
oak trees were mistletoe clumps. Rod said: "Don't shake
them down. Mistletoe poisons the sheep." Too shortly, we
were speeding on through the fields again. Randy gazed up
and saw a hawk floating effortlessly in the breeze. He said:
"It's not fair, it's just not fair," as he stretched out his arms
in aimless imitation.

When I worked in the gardens, an old priest, who looked
depressed, directed the projects. He spoke slowly and sadly
but had a zest for potted flowers and deep beds of shrubs. A
faint glimmer of a smile sometimes pierced his darkened face.
Another priest once asked him: "How are you, Father?" He
responded: "Most of the time it's bad and sometimes it's
worse."

My memories were interrupted by a call to "group."

About four times a week the ambulatory patients assembled for "group." Some days there were simple games, such as a trust dance in which two people started at opposite ends of a raised, narrow board, and had to slip around each other to the other side. You could manage the necessary dance step only if you held on and trusted the other person. Another game was pounding pillows and verbalizing anger. Another was role playing a cop and speeder in which the cop stopped a driver who did not think he was speeding. We had to be assertive in answering the cop, not aggressive—overreacting—nor passive—underreacting. Passivity was our normal reaction.

Another group exercise was selecting toys, driftwood, or games, and then explaining how the frog, or teddy bear, or turtle represented who I was. These activities helped us verbalize who we were and how we felt.

Two volunteers involved us in art work. One had us working in clay on Wednesdays. The other helped us make collages out of colored paper and cloth on Thursdays. I molded a turtle in clay to indicate my slow, persistent progress and my shell to shield my innards. I could never just do something; it had to symbolize something. The collage lady said my work was attractive and symbolic though she did not say what it symbolized.

On August 9th I wrote: "The group leader must be conscious of trying too hard. He or she may be forcing an issue, hedging one's own insecurity, or seeking reenforcement for one's self-image. As in prayer, a good group leader will have a sense for the tired of listening, trusting and relaxing in order to learn. It is good for the group leader to listen to the direction of the group or its problems before proposing anything. The second step is to establish an atmosphere of trust. This step may be arrived at slowly or quickly depending on the feelings of the group. It may involve casting out demons, that is, re-enforcing the good feelings which are already there."

I was always analyzing everything that was going on around me. Much of what happened I probably did not notice and my biggest blind spot was whatever was going on within me.

Day 36:

Some of the patients got on our nerves at times. We were tight to begin with, but one patient, Clarice, acted out every nervous twitch she had. Happily she was not in the ward very long. One day she said: "Ever since I got here I haven't had a decent meal. They always ignore what I put down."

Sara: "She's a perpetual motion machine. She's always running around in circles. It really bugs me."

Clarice (ignoring everyone): "They shut you all up. They don't tell you anything in this home of the free and land of the brave."

Ruth (staff person): "Have you made your bed yet, Clarice?"

Clarice: "No."

Ruth: "Don't you think you better start with that?"

Clarice: "Listen, honey. I've been making beds for 40 years, a lot longer than you. I'll get to it."

Another patient who perplexed us was Dottie, an aging Barbie doll. About 38, she was wound tighter than any person I had ever seen. Her face was carefully painted and veneered to save whatever cuteness remained, and she was shapely though verging, ever so slightly, on the plump side. We tried to get her to loosen up, but the veneer never cracked; she never exploded with the pent up, seething anger that all but steamed out of the hairline fissures in her face.

I could not see as well what was going on within me. Years of repression had preserved a narrow area of safety for myself. My outlet was to write, but my concentration was weak and notes were in fits and starts. Much of it was spent unraveling whatever had happened in that searing experience of the retreat.

Day 37:

The Lord's presence is in every living creature. The mysterious Spirit suffuses all creation, calls us to Christ through creation.

Music mirrors the joy of community and contributes to celebration. A symphony images the building up of the Body of Christ. I wonder how Arvesu would see all this?

I started to collect a few witty sayings and aphorisms from *Reader's Digest*. None of them had much logic or bearing on what was going on within me. A saying of Napoleon's about Metternik appealed to me: "He's a piece of dung in a silk stocking." I squirreled away another quote from Toynbee: "The Englishman's truly distinctive disease is his cherished habit of waiting until the 13th hour." Strands and bits of passing insights often flooded my imagination.

Several things made me fearful. For one, I disliked the medicine. At the same time I was afraid I would reach a point where the medicine would not work. My biggest fear by far was the possible recurrence of a psychotic episode. That rattled me. Initially I was given 400 mg. of Thorazine a day along with some Artane. The psychiatrist checked out the side effects regularly. This gave us a safe area to talk about.

Zieverink: How do you feel? Any rubberiness in your arms or legs?

Howell: Some. My arms feel like plastic twitching occasionally. Generally I feel fine. I'm taking long walks through the neighborhood. It's rather nice.

Zieverink: Be careful of the sun. One of the side effects of Thorazine is that you are more susceptible to sunburns. And, of course, we have already talked about your dryness in the mouth.

I was always super nervous when he came around. My mouth would dry to a desert waste; I wanted to make sure he knew I was recovering rapidly.

Zieverink: Any funny thoughts?

Howell: Like what? (I did not like his probing.)

Zieverink: Oh. Strange ideas. Things from the retreat?

Howell: Well, it's hard to separate it all out. I'm trying to process a few things. Keep in touch with how I'm feeling.

Zieverink: That's good. What are your thoughts about going home?

Howell: I won't have anything to do. I'll feel like a left thumb on a right hand.

Zieverink: We'll need to talk about that. When you get out, you will start seeing me. Here's a card with my address on it. Will you be able to get there all right?

Howell: I'll be able to drive, I guess.

Zieverink: O.K., we'll be keeping you here a few more days and then you'll be released.

Several months after I left the hospital, Dr. Zieverink dropped "tardive dyskinesia" on me, another long-term side effect. Patients who take heavy doses of anti-psychotic drugs, like Thorazine, can develop uncontrollable facial twitches and spasms after many years of use. No effective cures exist for these spasms though there are some treatments, one of which is to discontinue the drug which could allow a psychotic episode to occur. Ironically, another method is to increase the dosage heavily, which clears up the spasms. Obviously this method would have only short-term advantages, since it is precisely the heavy dosage of the drug which causes the spasms. Dr. Zieverink gave me only the minimal explanation at the time and even most of this did not register. My fear of disaster was acute, however. "Tardive dys . . . " I blotted out even the words.

"Tardive dyskinesia." My tongue stuck to my mouth and I rolled my lips. I could already feel a tick or twitch in my left eye. Spastic on top of being psychotic. I mistakenly thought the Artane I was taking helped to prevent these nerve spasms. Actually the Artane was for the Parkinson trembling, my rubbery stiffness, which occurred as a side effect in the initial stages of the Thorazine treatment.

Despite my fears of a breakdown occurring again, I was impatient to leave the hospital. Finally on August 13 Joe picked me up in a car to go back to Jesuit High. He was normally an extremely fast driver and that day was no different. Images and cars went went whizzing by me so rapidly I felt dizzy. Sensing a chance to use my assertive training, I asked him to slow down.

At Jesuit High, I felt I had landed in a foreign land which was vaguely familiar from the newsreels. I was faint, even weak physically. In the residence, the long narrow hallway with the dusty, pale purple carpet looked strangely familiar. *I did some bizarre things that week.* My room was mildly disturbed, just as I had left it. Scattered notes covered my desk.

I checked the sink to make sure it was clean; I did not want to leave a dirty sink for someone else to clean. A shirt was draped over the chair and the room looked as if someone had suddenly died; no one had quite gotten around to sifting through the personal effects.

December, 1982

> *Lo duca ed io per quel cammino ascoso*
> *entrammo a ritornar nel chiaro mondo;*
> *e, sanza cura aver d'alcun riposo,*
> *salimmo su, ei primo ed io secondo,*
> *tanto ch'io vidi delle cose belle*
> *che porta il ciel, per un pertugio tondo;*
> *e quindi uscimmo a riveder le stelle.*

Heck, Kuder, I thought you would recognize the last lines of the Inferno. *Remember when Dante finally gets through hell with Virgil. He goes out into the clear skies finally freed from the hellish torments that caused his tortured soul to faint. Then he sees the stars again before he starts his ascent up the Mount of Purgatory. Here's a translation for you:*

> *By that hid way my guide and I withal,*
> > *Back to the lit world from the darkened dens*
> > *Toiled upward, caring for no rest at all,*
>
> *He first, I following; till my straining sense*
> > *Glimpsed the bright burden of the heavenly call*
> > *Through a round hole; by this we climbed, and thence*
>
> *We forth, to look once more upon the stars.*

    Today's the winter solstice. The shortest day of the year. The Mass reading from a few days ago. "Drop down dew ye heavens and let the earth bring forth a Savior," always reminds me of Sheridan with all the rain or Jerusalem during Christmas. It always seems to rain in Bethlehem at Christmas time. That's when the hillside pastures finally turn green again.

    Lance reminds me of Howarth in that series on Masterpiece Theatre: ready caustic wit, shrewd observer of the passing scene among the school lads at a British prep school. He said last night: "The only thing the British preserved of the Greek Empire was hybris, *overweening pride."*

Chapter Six
A SLOW RECOVERY:
AUGUST, 1975 - MAY, 1976

I returned to the high school community in a daze, in a kind of caffeine high that had lasted too long. Upended and out of place, I was anxious to appear "well," to seem normal and ordinary. More importantly, I was dreadfully anxious that I not get sick again.

Another anxiety harried me even more. I wondered deep down whether I would be allowed to continue as a Jesuit. No one had said anything to me about it. This fear was my worst identity crisis since being a Jesuit was so crucial to who I was. Three factors heightened this fear: First of all, I could not work as a Jesuit. I was a castoff and useless in everything. Unemployed and unemployable, I had lost any personal esteem that went with productivity and usefulness. Secondly, I would probably never be able to make a retreat again. The risk of a psychosis while making a retreat was too great. However, such retreats were thoroughly intertwined with Jesuit identity since Ignatius had made the 30-day retreat the cornerstone of Jesuit spirituality. So my need to avoid a retreat confirmed by worst fear. Finally, I could not pray. The few times I attempted to pray I became agitated and strung out.

If I can just get my thoughts in order I'll be well again. If my memory weren't so lousy, I could sort out what I'm supposed to do and draw on all the things I've been told.

So my life was a shambles, stripped of coherence and purpose. Previous ambitions were shattered. I had no energy or resources to pull it all together. Not only had I crashed, but I had been abandoned by God who was remote and foreboding. He had raised me up and let me fall with a resounding thump. My friends did not know how to react and so said little or nothing, figuring that was the safer course.

Three Jesuits were, however, a huge support. Kevin was available any time day and night that I wanted to talk. Though I was reticent to talk much, he was a sturdy pillar. Jim, the rector, responded well to whatever I asked and had one basic message: "Do whatever the doctor says." Finally I had been surprised and pleased when my old friend from Rome, Steve, had been assigned to the school. Mike, the president of the school, had requested a Jesuit to work in campus ministry, giving retreats, and teaching religion to compensate for my loss from the school. So in late July the provincial assigned Steve to Jesuit High. These three—Steve, Jim, and Kevin—were a lifeline of support which enabled me to make feeble steps forward.

One evening, about a week after I returned to the high school, six of us went out to dinner. A California Jesuit, Mike, had just returned from Rome and held forth on Vatican politics. Evidently Pope Paul VI vetoed the recommendations of the Jesuit General Pedro Arrupe for the new rector of the Gregorian University and chose to have the current rector continue for another three years. Mike felt that the Pope did not place his full confidence in Arrupe. Rather he trusted Fr. Paolo Dezza, a former Jesuit General Assistant and an Italian. This choice made for confused lines of authority, even though Arrupe made every effort to follow the wishes of the Pope. *If they could straighten out the lines of obedience then the church could get its act together. Just like when Catherine of Siena finally straightened out the Pope and reformed the church. Don Quixote was a reformer too, just like Ignatius without the gallop, tilt and windmills. Maybe I'll be called to Rome as a discerner to straighten out the mess.* I was getting anxious as Mike talked about Rome and I tensed, almost in a panic, from these racing ideas.

My strongest strand of hope was the twice-weekly sessions with Dr. Zieverink. Shortly after my hospitalization I approached a stuccoed, vine-covered two-story house. The vines were just starting to turn red and orange. A sprinkler sputtered vainly to cover the grass with water, and from the side of the house I spotted two apple trees with bruised-looking apples. Through the trees I caught a glimpse of downtown Portland with Mt. Hood in the hazy blue east. I entered through the wooden door and told the dullish receptionist who I was, before I sat down on the far edge of a drab couch. The room was dark. A Mozart symphony that I could not place sounded over an adequate stereo system. On the floor at the knees of her mother was a squirming, plumpish girl of nine. Her bedraggled mother allowed her free rein to romp around the room. I did not know which one was going to see the psychiatrist. Shortly, a weasle-looking doctor came down the stairs and called out, "Margot." The girl straightened up and, ignoring her mother, eagerly greeted the doctor. I was glad I was not going to see him.

Just then Dr. Zieverink skipped on down the steps and called, "Pat." I followed him up the steps and entered a large room. A desk, piled with papers and books, adjoined the door. A large chair, a lamp, and a couch were at the other end. A few nondescript paintings hung on the wall. I later commented on the lack of color, except for a couple of plants. Zieverink said it was deliberate so as not to arouse the imagination or projections of the patient. We sat down on the two chairs by the desk, where the room was more structured. Zieverink stuffed his pipe and gazed quietly at me as he drew deeply and lit his pipe with a lighter. My mouth was dry, so I asked for a glass of water. I hated talking about myself. "How are things going?" he asked. I told him that I believed the illness was going to be a healing process for me. "I get uptight when I talk to people. But now I can practice some of the relaxation techniques I learned in the hospital to relieve tension." "Who do you get uptight with?" "Almost anyone." Already I was tensing. I did not really want to be here. If I could just walk out of here "all well," I would not have to go through these tortuous sessions. I felt helpless, humiliated and trapped. *It's too deep. He'll never get at the illness. I can't talk about these things. They're too personal.* "One shouldn't hang out the family wash," my father said. "What we say here at the table is confidential." *I wonder if he's going to grill me about my sex life or lack of it?*

Z asked me some questions about Peter's death and the "living death" of leprosy in Molokai. Evidently we had talked about it once before. I did not remember I had told him this. Z said something about suppressing things. Or was it repressing? I could never keep them straight. We talked about leprosy. "Cleansing of leprosy is frequent in the Bible, isn't it?" Zieverink asked. *I wonder if he's Jewish. He looks Jewish. All he needs is a yarmulke for his head to go with his brownish beard. Can you really cleanse your feelings and memory? Maybe that could straighten out my head, I mean my imagination.*

"What are you thinking?" Zieverink said.

"Oh, nothing." My mind registered a zero. *Was that suppression or repression?* What I had been thinking faded like a dream.

We talked about how I was getting along. For the time being I was sorting through some old notes, making plans to go home to Minnesota in a couple weeks, and I had been invited or told, I do not know which, to work on school publicity and recruiting. I told him one of the freshmen withdrew from school the first week because Jesuit High was "too Catholic." The parents said: "We knew it was Catholic, but we didn't know it was *that Catholic.*" Another freshman came into the office the first day of school bewildered. In tears he sighed: "My schedule says I have first and second lunch periods, but I only brought one lunch with me." Our session seemed inconclusive. Z said the healing would take a long time.

I started to rummage through some old notes from Weston, Massachusetts, where I had studied philosophy 1964 to

1966. I was sifting through the past, looking for bedrock.

Here's a good one by Josef Pieper. A peeping Joe!
"Justice is the more excellent part of the soul. It is the inner-
most kernel of the spiritual will and it directs all the other vir-
tues." Justice is like trust. You need it for healing. Here's a
good one by Chesterton, a paradox. A pair of ox? Should be
a paradoxen. "A fairy tale discusses what a sane man will do
in a mad world. The sober realistic novel of today discusses
what an essential lunatic will do in a dull world." Let's see
now where was I? Oh, Chesterton. "Mysticism keeps men
sane. As long as you have mystery, you have health; when
you destroy mystery you create morbidity." Mystery is light
inaccessible. I went beyond the limits and found the dark
demon.

Weston was a relief from Sheridan; it was like going into a
foreign country. A new language. Charlie chuckled when my
Oregon friend John asked him how many head of beef we
had here at Weston. John was serious too. Of course, he used
to wander through the Sheridan pasture talking to those
brown-eyed beasts. We were a little parochial. They thought
John had a Western accent and I talked like the newscasters.
"That's Standard American that you find around the Great
Lakes." "I'm blue blood of North Dakota, you know. My
grandfather was the first white boy born in Oakes, North
Dakota. He used to lead the parades when I was a kid."

George and I canvassed the black neighborhood of Rox-
bury for a local parish. A fetid stench seeped up through the
dog-manured streets around the housing district. A black
lady said an aborted fetus had been found in the garbage can
the week before. George seemed to take all this better than I
did. Some flowers bloomed in the street, even in the pave-
ment cracks. Carl Jung said: "Life is like a plant that lives on
its rhizome. Its true life is invisible, hidden in the rhizome.
The part that appears above ground lasts only a single sum-

mer. What we see is the blossom, which passes, the rhizome remains." I'm unearthing my archetypal rhizome through Memories, Dreams and Retreats.

Of the many memorable events that occurred at Weston, I recalled an excursion with George. In those days before Vatican II ended, we were still regimented. Our TV watching was restricted. We all wore cassocks, the infrequent visits home were for a single day and money was doled out a few dollars at a time. The one excursion you could get permission for was to visit the Boston Fine Arts Museum. So one day George, my lean Connecticut Yankee friend, and I "got permission for the Museum" and then headed into town to see the movie, "The Pawnbroker." We were both moved by the movie which depicted a Jew in New York who had flashbacks to his days in a Nazi concentration camp. The pawnbroker, played by Rod Steiger, extorts money from miserable, trapped folks, and he himself is caught in a web of crime and exploitation. In a poignant flash he realizes how he oppresses the poor as he himself had been in the camp. After that crucifixion of awareness, he plunges his hand through a paper spindle. The movie ends with his groping to communicate his agony to his family. George and I were silent after the movie. Thoughts of suffering mixed with nostalgia coursed through my mind and left a residue of peace. It was better to be aware of one's injustices and interior agony, rather than blind and stolid, even if it could not be communicated with others. My defenses were down, my interior censor collapsed in the July retreat. I was a ship being lowered in the locks and passed along through the checkpoints to the next lower and more dangerous level. Finally image after image flooded over me. Would I never come up for air?

At the end of August, I planned to go home to my parents who were now living in Detroit Lakes, Minnesota. When I said goodbye to Zieverink, I said I could get through it O.K. and I owed it to them to let them know I was all right. When I arrived, they were delighted to see me and concerned although we did not talk about the breakdown. They hoped that I would do whatever I wanted to do while I was home. I went golfing with my brother Mike and, for a change, he did not correct my swing.

When I visited my Grandma Mikkelson in the rest home, it reminded me of the psych ward. A big sign was at the entrance: "Today is Tuesday, September 2. It is windy outside." *When you're old, you're distorted too. Hearing and sight go awry. Memory fails. At least it doesn't smell here. Grandma and I are both frail, but she's at the end and I'm at the beginning.* Zieverink has been asking me about my family. Now many of the pieces seemed to flow together as my mother, my grandmother and I said the rosary together.

"What's your family like? Tell me about them," Zieverink said.

My dad is quiet and reserved, except at a party where he loves to tell stories. All the Howells are quiet. In 1890 my Grandfather Lou Howell came from South Bend, Indiana, to Sheldon, North Dakota, or rather Ransom County, to homestead on 160 acres and build a sod cabin. He froze that first winter, dug a shelter in the snow bank along the Sheyenne River. Lou Howell didn't say much. He had come from Indiana with his cousin who was a Metzger. Everyone in Sheldon thought my grandfather's name was Lou Metzger and he never corrected them until his third month in town when a check arrived from South Bend made out to Lou Howell. Then he had a helluva time straightening out who he was before he could cash the check. My Grandmother Howell was also quiet, but stern. She taught Mike and me how to play cards when we were five and six. At one point she got impatient with us and scolded us: "If you can't play right, you shouldn't play at all." We loved having her around, though, because she taught us how to play dominos, Chinese checkers and engaging card games.

My dad, the youngest of four children, was born at home on March 3, 1910. He was subject to the same loving sternness that we would later receive from his mother. My grandfather instilled in him a horse sense for business. During Prohibition in the 20s my grandfather was the main Sheldon outlet for "home brew." The liquor was shipped by rail from Canada, through Staples, Minnesota, to his lumber yard. Naturally my grandmother didn't think much of this line of business, but she did her best to ignore it as long as it was done in my grandfather's domain at the lumber yard.

Grandma was a convert to Catholicism. A descendant of an itinerant Spiritualist minister and solid Scotch-Irish Presbyterians who took religion seriously, she laced her love for Catholicism and her judgment of the various pastors with strains of unacknowledged Calvinism. For many years she did the altar linens for the Church although at one point she got into a tiff with the pastor and not only quit her voluntary service, but refused to go to Church for over a year. She was as stubborn as quack grass.

Sheldon was only 20 miles from our home in Lisbon. One of our periodic treats was to take the train from Lisbon to Sheldon to see Grandma. Mike and I were never bored at Grandma Howell's. Once we finished playing baseball with the neighbors, we picked strawberries under her watchful eye, or she pulled out the ice cream maker. We churned the creamy mixture round the crushed ice and rock salt until our arms collapsed.

My interest was piqued when she washed clothes. I drew the water from the old-fashioned pump at the side sink in the kitchen, and then I watched her carve slivers of Ivory soap or Fels Naptha into the stained metal tubs. I am sure she considered it all very modern when she first did it "up brown" in 1910, but it looked terribly quaint in 1950.

Everything seemed old and historical and I savored her

stories. She told of her own mother, Great Grandma Freeman, as a girl of 16. The girls then—about 1860—wore steel-
hooped skirts to the barn dances. But on a rainy, stormy
night they would be afraid of being hit by lightning, so after
the dance they would sneak out back to slip out of the hoops
and tuck them safely away. Grandma Freeman fell in love
with my great grandfather when she was 16. When he rode
off to the Battle of Gettysburg, she thought he was "the
handsomest man she had ever seen." They were married as
soon as he returned home after the Civil War.

I felt I was sneaking back through history, like rummaging
through an old attic with trunksful of treasured letters, old
stamps, pressed flowers and wedding mementoes. The
women preserved the stories, the men talked more about the
politics and business of the day.

My mother is more expressive, religious and emotionally
supportive than my father. Grandpa Mikkelson was Danish
and also a convert to Catholicism. Grandma Mikkelson was a
Ryan and militantly Irish Catholic. Together they raised ten
children. My mother was born September 3, 1916, the third of
the ten. My Mikkelson grandparents farmed three miles out of
town. Mom walked to town or ran to school with her dog
Shep, ever-faithful friend and protector. A great storyteller,
my mother enchanted us with tales about two horses, old Bell,
a steady Belgian work horse, and Trixie, a well-named riding
horse that loved to go racing for the barn, head low, and speed
through a low door to scrape the rider off her back.

My mother told how when my grandpa got a new car, a
1937 Packard, all the family piled in for a ride. After a short
run, they returned to the farm and got out. Grandpa was
backing it up to a trailer hitch when my young uncle yelled
out, "Whoa!" and my grandfather, who had driven horses
for 20 years, responded as if he had a pair of reins in his
hands and pulled the steering wheel right out of the shaft.

My memories of the Mikkelson's are filled with a welter of

40 first cousins, huge Thanksgiving Day feeds, endless romps through the fields, races with the chickens and a constant swirl of laughter, cooking and stories.

Mother was especially close to her brother Tom. They teased each other mercilessly. At one point my mother was dating someone named Romeo. Tom mocked her role as Juliet: "Romeo, Romeo, wherefore art thou," he would chant on bended knee. The Mikkelsons made it clear whether they approved of your fiance or not. My uncle's girlfriend from Boston and my aunt's boyfriend Cain, whom the family promptly dubbed "Sugar," met similar fates. Romeo did not last. Before too many years Joe Howell was visiting the farm. He held a good hand at cards and enjoyed the Mikkelson stories, so they thought he was smart, a quiet man with a fine sense of humor.

My parents had met at the Silver Zephyr, a dance hall near Lisbon, the town where they both worked. Dancing was forever after a hallmark of the Howells. When I was growing up, we had relatives all around us. A short trip in the car, even on a wintry day, and we were surrounded with a larger family and good times. My mother thought my dad was "a very good man," smart and kind. She liked the fact that he was a Catholic. When my dad went to confession just before he was married and explained to the priest that he was marrying Virginia Mikkelson, the pastor warned him about those Scandinavian Lutherans, unaware of my mother's tenacious Irish Catholic roots.

They were married in Oakes on September 5, 1939, a few days after Hitler marched into Poland to begin World War II. My mother panicked briefly before the ceremony, but Grandma Mikkelson shook that out of her. She said firmly: "Joe's a fine man and you'll be very happy." All in all, she was right.

After the wedding, the fun began. No Mikkelson wedding was complete then or since without a shivaree, an old-

fashioned "roast" of the bride and groom. My mother's brothers and sisters outfitted an empty hay wagon with a park bench to which they tied a billy goat, then enthroned the folks on the bench, and paraded them through the town with great honking of horns, fireworks and shouts of glee. I was later to witness many similar weddings. The bridal car usually took the brunt of it. The pranksters would hide the wheels, or stuff a potato up the exhaust which choked off the engine, or fill the hubcaps with marbles, or secret a chicken in the back seat of the car. After his initiation, no one enjoyed this tomfoolery, kidding, and teasing more than my dad. His quiet mask came unglued when he would join the Mikkelsons, and he became just as boisterous as any maternal uncle.

They honeymooned at Detroit Lakes, Minnesota, in a cabin owned by Dad's uncle, Colonel Carroll, a surviving veteran of the Civil War. From there they drove to the Black Hills in South Dakota. At Mt. Rushmore Dad nicknamed my mother, "my wild prairie rose," the sweetest thing that grows. The four presidential visages were being sculpted out of the mountain that year.

Dad worked for Frank Dills, a local Rexall druggist, in a store built about 1890. Hours were long and tedious—from 8 a.m. to 10 p.m. weekdays with every other Sunday off. He calculated he was earning about 25 cents per hour when he first started working. My mother was soon pregnant, and even before, Dad insisted that she give up her job so that she could be the proper housewife. Mother spent a quiet, rather boring, first year in which she occupied herself with much knitting and crocheting and preparing for the new baby.

These thoughts of a happier, simpler time often preoccupied me while I was home that fall. In fact, I spent a fair amount of time with my parents asking them questions about the old days.

How did I get to this impasse? Was I still seeking parental

approval in an infantile, compulsive way? As I laid on the dock languidly rocking in the waves, I gazed back at my parents' home on the shore. My father, now in his retirement, was mowing the grass, a favorite occupation second only to chopping wood. Mother's daisies and geraniums huddled around the deck in front of the picture window. "We just want you to be happy. Is there anything we can do?" I shrugged it off and rolled over to gaze up at the pillowed sky. There's no bootstrap cure, but where do you start?

When I returned to Portland, I was able to say Mass again. When I read Scripture, my mind did not start buzzing or skip around from text to text. After my time at home I felt better; a slight amount of control returned and my thoughts no longer seemed to race around with frightening speed. My visit had drained away a few of my fears. These feelings did not carry over when I saw Zieverink in his vine-covered, stucco house office. Our conversation was direct but never so terse as I would remember it afterwards:

"How'd the visit go?"

"O.K." I was nervous and dry-mouthed.

"What did your parents have to say?"

"Not much."

"Were they concerned about you?"

"I think so."

"What did they say about your breakdown?"

"We didn't talk about it."

"What did you talk about?"

"Not much" (long silence). Zieverink stares at me.

"What are you thinking?"

"Oh, nothing."

"You really don't want to be here, do you?"

"Well, I need to get well."

"And, you're still sick?"

"I feel it. I don't have any control."

Our conversations went like this for many weeks. I could

not pierce the surface of my feelings. Nothing emerged except
an enduring ache and pain and frustration. At the end of the
session with Zieverink, I said:

"I'm totally frustrated. Nothing's happening."

"That's the way it is sometimes. See you Thursday."

Afterwards I felt better. I did not know why. At the next
session I was more involved. He seemed like he cared about
what I was feeling. Perhaps that was it. I said: "I think all
this is a sign for better things in the future, but it's very unnerving now."

That day I wrote a short article for the Jesuit school
newspaper, saw a student photographer about taking some
pictures, and cleaned out my files in the principal's office. If I
was angry about not being principal, I was not aware of it. I
cleaned out my files and got out of the way. Later I said 5
o'clock Mass for a few people. I felt during this time that I
could not do anything on my own, that I had to trust in
others yet. Faith offered no solace, only confusion. God
might as well be dead.

*The dead cannot praise Yahweh. They have gone down to
silence. From my darkened pit I'm chastened, Lord. I can
hardly cry "Lord" without a churning in my gut. Yet You are
with me in my distress. Return to your resting place. Our
hearts are restless until they rest in you, but you're a wan-
derer yourself, an alien god who's fickle. Yet I know you're
not. My own idols have eyes that see not, ears that hear not,
and mouths that speak not. I am my own idol. Let me die and
be rescued. Relieve me from my despair, from my roving anxiety, and from myself.*

My encounters with Zieverink were the focus of my week. I
sped down the highway, walked through the rustling, golden
leaves to the stucco house, and entered the dark reception
room. I glanced through *National Geographic* and listened to
the aimless chatter of Margot and her disheveled mother.
Finally I would see Zieverink and we would talk, listen and

talk. Little is memorable. He did a good deal of the talking himself. I am sure 80 percent of his energy was spent in getting me to open up. Afterwards I would try to reflect on all we had said.

Personal acceptance is the condition of reacting objectively. Great idea. Who said it? He hit the jackpot, but did he do it himself? Labels are great, but what is really going on?

My envy of the new principal went unchecked. I resented his arrogance. I did not want to be envious or resentful, but I had to admit that I was. He belittled everything that had happened last year.

Zieverink said I should titrate my medicine, that is, spread it out and take it as I needed it. He also said to take it as a prophylactic or preventive measure. He used these medical terms as if I knew exactly what they meant. His assumption flattered me. I was beginning to relax more. Cutting back on coffee reduced my jitteriness.

My thoughts tended towards Rome as they had many times before. The possibility of studies there next year was suggested by the rector, Jim. When I mentioned this to Zieverink, he strongly advised against it. "You need a capable health support system." I must have repressed this attraction to Rome because my reactions were mild and receptive compared to the depth of my desires.

Ideas on decisionmaking and discernment confused me. *Lord, you lead me and you guide me, but you sure write with crooked lines. Augustine says, "Narrow is the mansion of my soul." Amen to that. Enlarge it so that you can enter swiftly and heal me at my broken depth. Dredge the ash and dust from this stream so that your grace may flow once more within me.*

I kept pouring over the experiences of the past summer. I was trying to solve the problem of my breakdown by analyzing every bit and chunk. If I could just figure out the reasons for the breakdown, then perhaps I would be well again. Much

of my ambivalence arose from my religious experience. I said
with Teresa of Avila: "Lord, if this is the way you treat your
friends, no wonder you have so few of them." *Lord, you de-*
ceived me. How can I even say the words? I was deluded.
From whence did it come, but from you. No friend would
continue to stab me in the back and kick me in the groin. The
saints are gone. We will never see them again as we once did.
They were all psychotic.

Lillian, the psychiatric nurse, had said that St. Therese,
the Little Flower and St. Ignatius were both psychotics. Their
religious imagination took over their being. They offered
themselves so completely to the Lord that they became much
like Christ. Though their religious experience was important,
what resulted from this experience was far more significant.

Lord, I'm back again. I don't know why. You're the only
one I can talk to. I'm not saying that you understand. At least
I haven't seen that part of it yet. I've seen suffering, fear, and
more fear. I tried once to surrender myself to you, but you
seduced me and dumped me. Words of prayer don't come to
me. I'm too numb. Give me your hand. Give me a glimpse of
your face, but not all of it. I need a touch of life, something
to give me hope in this gloomy vale. "Lord, help me!" I am
drowning.

Waves of my retreat in July kept rolling in. I was uneasy
with their strength which, like the rising tide, surged at the
pillars at my feet. I knew that religious experience could have
pathological origin and yet have a value. From the sickness of
the mind could arise luminous, reasonable and helpful experiences. Religious experience and mental disorder are par-
allel. Both can entail a great emotional crisis and both can
mean the mind's attempt to reorganize itself. The measure
and interpretation of the crisis are found in the success or

failure of the reorganization. When the outcome is successful the experience will be called religious. Where it is unsuccessful, it will be labeled pathological.

No one event or experience of God would define my life. Rather the history of my life lived out day to day in the struggle to be kind and faithful to others would interpret what had happened.

Much anxiety continued to flow through me. One of my constant fears was that I could never pray again. Whenever I attempted contemplative prayer, my thoughts raced again. I would grow tense and fearful. What little prayer I did had to be concrete: a quick examen or reflection on the day, a decade of the rosary, a little Scripture and daily Mass. None of my interior experiences were prayer.

My quiet moments were spent reflecting on my past, on my current feelings, and how the day was going. I was learning to cope with emotions, and despite much resistance from me, Zieverink was helping to see a few links between my present behavior and my past.

Gradually it dawned on me that all these psychological issues were a context for prayer. I was heartened when I saw that this struggle was now my own unique prayer. In this prayer I ran my finger over the events of the day, probing for emotional responses. Wherever there was pain or reaction, I dwelled on it to decipher what was occurring. Through this patient prayer I knew the Lord was reknitting my life together.

Your healing is not magic. It works in and through me and through all the gifts of people you surround me with. The building up of your body brings peace to others. Hasten your coming. Heal me at the depths so that I can once more praise and serve you.

In October I started thinking about the future. I needed to escape this squirrel cage. I was drawn to further studies, especially on the *Spiritual Exercises,* Scripture and the integration of both with psychology. Was I attracted to my greatest weakness?

At times the Thorazine made me groggy and forgetful. The forgetfulness signaled a lack of control. *Let me do something. Have you led me down this dusty, ash-strewn path for nothing? You could have left me stumbling along as I was, giving you dumb praise. This fragile search for healing is a humiliation. Why did this illness occur? Where do I go from here?*

During that fall I worked with Steve to give student retreats or days of recollection in groups of 30 at the Jesuit retreat house. My responsibilities were minimal since Steve led all the discussions. Occasionally I celebrated the liturgy. Steve took the students through a "spirit walk" or hypnotic dream state prayer, with the song "Morning has Broken" as background.

> Morning has broken
> Like the first morning,
> Blackbird has spoken
> Like the first bird.
> Praise for the singing!
> Praise for the morning!
> Praise for them, springing
> Fresh from the Word!

A big raucous bird hovered in the dawn eyeing the crisp dew-hung trees. The light blinded me so that the bird's beak poked my eyes. My dawn was a long ways off. Bring your recreation of the new day.

October 9, 1975. Fr. Jack Leary, an old friend and mentor from my university days, phoned: "We should get together. How about dinner some place?" Balding and splotchy from the California sun, he radiated a joy at our getting together. His wit pierced through the years of separation and turmoil

that had marked both our lives. He rose above his own em-
broilments with past ghosts and sparkled with humor and an
Irish penchant for dressing up a story in its best possible
guise. "Kevin says, 'You are one of the most sensitive people
he knows.' " Aware of the compliment, I still felt weakened
by it. I had to be on my guard since Jack discussed all his
friends with everyone else. "People are more enlightened
these days about mental illness. It's not the stigma it used to
be," he observed in his didactic style. I loosened up as he
reeled off what he had been doing. Sensing his approval and
support, I felt a melancholic strain. I pined for a calmer,
more joyful day, when I felt secure. Jack's visit gave me a
fleeting glimpse of this. Zieverink and I sorted out some of
my feelings in a lengthy dialogue:

"A good friend of mine was in town and we went out to
dinner."

"Good. What did you talk about?"

"Not too much. Old times and a bit about me," I said
weakly.

"Like what?"

"He's the first one who really asked me how I was doing
and seemed to understand what was going on."

"Are you relieved or angry about it?"

"I wish there were someone around I could talk to." I
squirmed in my chair.

"What about Kevin?"

"Oh, yeah. We do, but that's different."

"What's different?"

"Well, we joke around and he understands, but we don't
talk much about what's really going on."

"So how was it different with Jack?"

"Jack asked the right questions and heard the answers. It
was O.K. to be sick."

"So he showed concern for you." He leaned forward
intently.

"And I felt all right. I could relax a bit, instead of being uptight talking about myself."

"Does this remind you of anything else? Or anyone else?"

"It used to be that way with Mike, my boss. I felt good about working with him."

"Then what happened?"

"We grew apart when I became principal. He thought I should have more independence and the president shouldn't interfere with the principal."

"How did you feel about that?"

"Oh, I don't know. Maybe, isolated."

"So you had to do it all by yourself. You were no longer a young man, but an independent adult who had to make his own decisions."

"Something like that."

"Is this anything like what you said about your father?"

"Probably."

"How did you get along with your father?"

"I already told you last month," I said stiffly.

"Maybe you can tell me something more. Can you recall how it was?"

"O.K."

"O.K. Were you close to him?"

"He was around a lot because I worked at the drugstore for him and it was a small town."

"When was this?"

"1948 to 1958. When I was about eight and later."

"So what did you talk to him about?"

"Not much. He was pretty quiet around me. We'd talk about money sometimes. I would have to start the conversation. Maybe ask him a question."

"About what?"

"Oh, I don't know."

"So did you do any things together?"

"When I was young, we went hunting a lot. We did a lot of

pheasant hunting, but then when I was old enough to hunt myself, he had lost interest in hunting."

"We played a lot of cards. Mike and I played whist with the folks. Then they taught us how to play bridge when I was 12; Mike was 11. I begged Mom to teach us how to play and she finally agreed."

"We had some good times on trips until Dad would get tired. We went out West together a couple of times and when I was a sophomore, Mike and I and the folks went to a Mardi Gras in New Orleans. It's about the only thing I remember about my sophomore year."

"O.K. That's enough for today."

It all seemed inconclusive. Why talk about all this? Dad says: "Never hang out the wash in public." Steve and I used to joke about that; he had some great yarns about his own family. Privacy was easier; frankness came back to haunt you.

I assembled a slide show for the recruitment of eighth graders, part of my minimal duties as administrative adjunct around the school. About mid-October the Board of Directors of the high school viewed and critiqued the show. They wanted more of a "winner's" philosophy portrayed in the school. I felt tongue-tied. I could not rebut them and a flow of negative tension poured through me. Their values were contrary to mine; my anger surged. After showing it 20-25 times during the next couple months to various eighth-grade groups, I was so sick of it myself I could not stomach the contents.

I'm back to ground zero. Nothing turns out. This daily dying is endless. Maybe that's what I imagined in the July retreat. Your death was "ephapax," once for all, not an endless, cyclic dying and rising. Heal my broken body, flesh and all, so that you somehow live in me. My days are brown and gray, flat and sterile. No life blooms in this desert and sand clings to my tongue.

I kept a journal with sketches of what was occurring

around me. In mid-November I wrote: "The great advantage of Z is that he keeps me honest. He ferrets out my demons and circles round the beast to drive him out. My homily yesterday on selfish fear was well received, especially by the Jesuits. I cater to them. I was anxious about what I was going to say; then I realized my anxiety was coming from: 1) feelings of loneliness: no one understood what I was going through; 2) feelings of anger: I had not been included in decisions regarding the principalship for next semester; 3) feelings of certain people "not being there" when I needed them most. A combination of sadness and joy, linked to earlier childhood experiences.

November 18. I saw Z again today. The healing process seemed as slow as molasses in winter. Today we were beating a dead horse.

"How do you deal with these feelings of resentment, frustration and anger? Is it cricket to talk these out in the Society?" Zieverink probed.

"I don't have anyone to talk to about anger, though I did before Dave was transferred to Missoula."

"So what do you do now?"

"I find anger, even when I realize it, a rather uncreative emotion." Z gave me a little discourse on anger and then we talked about my plans for studies and for tertianship.

He said: "I'm still skeptical about your capacity for a 30-day retreat since quite frankly the altered state of the retreat had such dire results."

Afterwards I drove through Washington Park in the West Hills. The park was draped in cool, clear autumnal splendor. From every angle of the road as I wound up the hill, Mt. Hood shone in icy majesty. A few joggers puffed along the road with a flagging dog trotting along. The rough-hewn blocked stones circled the swan-lake reservoir. Two stranded ducks paddled round the winter cage. My car churned up leaves strewn in masses along the gutters. The yellow brick road. Other leaves clung to almost naked limbs, "bare ruin'd choirs, where late the sweet birds sang." One tree in yellow incandescence brightened the darkening shadows. The Italians would say, *incantevole,* so wonderful it is beyond singing.

My concentration was returning so I started reading again. Monika Hellwig in *Tradition* said that prayer and tradition have to be personalized and made fresh again: Prayer has to be in a spirit of search. It should be a means of breakthrough to a personal appropriation of one's religious heritage. It should lead to renunciation that serves to sharpen and correct one's personal focus, that sets one free to look at an issue afresh without interference from self-interest.

I thought she was not radical enough. This conversion sounded too safe, couched in tradition and protected by authority.

I started to write sketches of characters based on incidents around the school. I wrote about Steve with whom I was working each day: "A loose, dark red Pendleton shirt clung to his bulky frame. He was quiet, reserved. He liked to have the complete answer in his head before he said anything. Head atilt, his eyes would scan the ceiling and he could begin his discourse with, 'It appears to me . . . ' and at times it would seem as though something had appeared, as though he were reading from a TV prompter so well-honed and carefully scanned were his words. What he said, though, was never so trivial as a commercial, unless he were telling a joke. Then he would appear even more somber than usual, except that his eyes would start to twinkle. The joke or anecdote could easily be on himself and then he was apt to say: 'When I was in regency I taught Latin and thought I was a damned good teacher. Then I started teaching theology, the nemesis of all teachers. Yesterday I was boring them silly. I know now that I'm a shitty teacher.' "

I imagined myself as a writer at a party.

"Why do you write?" someone asked me.

"For the hell of it."

"No, I mean what do you get out of it?"

"Peace with myself; that's all. Certainly no money. And the readers could take a leap. I don't give a damn about them. They are sycophants, chewing up my soul. Oh, you do get the real readers; the pure ones, though, are science fiction readers. They put their own soul into it. They are almost like the writer. They expend themselves without much return, except peace."

"So what do you write about? What's your kick?"

He was asking dumb questions like I usually do, but I answered anyway. "No plot. We are always on the move. Why the hell does a book always have to have a plot. Readers, maybe the writers really, can't sustain interior action."

These exercises in writing tapped a deeper well where I felt at peace and away from the surface conflicts that absorbed my attention.

My love is fragile, like the maiden's, but pining for the lover. Lovers laugh at nonsense poetry. Their love is free; they don't cling to it but can see its ridiculous quality. Help my sense of humor. Wipe away the tears and bring your merriment.

December 6. The question of my job for next semester was fast approaching. I approached the acting principal with some careful queries. He pushed back his mop of hair. Was it a wig? He said: "Some of the faculty thought you should have been assigned to another school. They said you should never be principal again. Your credibility is gone. Some said: 'I won't tell him what I really think.' " He leaned forward earnestly and said: "That's not fair. It's like Senator Eagleton, though people don't know how to handle it." Trying to be responsive, I said: "Some of it is fear. People don't know how to handle severe mental illness." I left the principal's office wondering: Was he being supportive or manipulative?

The recovery had been like swimming up from 20 fathoms of water. Just as I began to surface and to come up gasping for air, I had to begin anew to swim through another 20 fathoms. Often I did not know if I were surfacing or plunging in this topsy-turvy world of depth darkness.

I sorted out my confusion through writing: "Creativity and courage are the ability to etch out one's life from an amorphous void. A creative person can give shape and sustenance to his life and transform emptiness into a quest for meaning. The past then stretches out into an intricate pattern of redeemed moments in time. To go forward, however, requires courage from within. The past, even a past full of accomplishments, cannot grant or ensure courage. That comes from within."

You unzipped me. You let me go through this tortuous illness. I need that faith which is the "courage to accept acceptance." I cringe before the pain that faces me. Grant me this courageous faith. Accept me as I am and let me be free of these hounds that gnaw within me.

December 11, 1975. I was now gainfully *unemployed!* I sensed I would never be principal again. The ground had shifted, the rules were changed. Everything was hunky dory with the new team of administrators. I was the sixth man on this well-knit basketball team and benched where I belonged. *Here's your old unprofitable servant. I'm clinging to my past and what I had. Where are you leading me? Down the primrose path? Haven't you destroyed enough already, must you lay siege to this last stronghold, my last shred of dignity?*

When a person is condemned, his creativity and power to love are broken. When he is accepted, there is sunshine and song. He is a new person, a new creation. Lord, give me this new birth. Be born again in me this Christmas. Help me to give up my clinging to power and security. Wean me from my job as principal, but do it quickly and without more pain.

December 13, 1975. I had three related dreams. The most vivid one was of a woman with reddish hair who floated over the sea with pleas of help. I was standing, looking out of a picture window on the second floor of our home in Lisbon. I invited her in. I tried to speak French to her, but she did not understand. Then I tried Italian, which she knew. *"Lei parla l'italiano?" "Si. Benissimo." "E cosi via."* Then her whole family came in. In the midst of this confusion, I dreamed of a reunion with my long-lost father in which I cried at length and my mother stood by crying also. The final dream was one in which I was outside a large castle compound. I paid 100 lire to a portly man to open the large double gates with a key. I was entering into a large enclosed area of myself.

December 16, 1975. Mike and Jim, the president and rector of the school, talked to Zieverink on Friday; Mike saw me afterwards. He explained a number of things about what had happened after I got sick. He said: "When you got sick last July, I fully thought in August that you would be the principal again in January. As time went along, though, things developed differently. It has nothing to do with you. It is just that the new team worked well together, and I think the new man has a terrific way with kids. He really is an experienced principal. He has really been a principal for four years now with Holy Child and the Tree of Learning. He knows more about education than either you or I do. It is not that I want to hurt you in any way, and I'm sorry if I have."

I agreed coolly that the new principal was excellent with kids but said that I thought he was rather weak with faculty and that my concern was that the Jesuit goals and Catholic quality of the school would suffer. He would direct it towards being a private prep school. I felt Mike had done the best he could but was trapped by circumstances. We then jogged over to his sister's place in the dark, foggy night.

I had been, to put it baldly, fired from my job.

Zieverink settled back in his chair. "We really haven't talked much about it from that perspective—that you were fired. How do you feel about that?"

"Frustrated in five ways! If I hadn't been sick I would still be principal."

"Possession is nine-tenths of the law."

"Yes. I am also ambivalent about my relationship with Mike. I have been without any work to do for two weeks, so there is some insecurity associated with that. What I have come to believe, though, is that I am now in a position to question in depth what I want to do with my life. I now have the freedom to make an honest choice. The principal's job was a crutch. It gave me a false sense of security. And it wasn't necessarily all that glamorous. At times I was just a glorified secretary. I would like to project myself in areas which are creative and related more directly with people. This insight is related to the retreat experience."

"Oh. I didn't know there had been a connection."

"Yes. Part of the conflict in the retreat was one between clutching to the security of what I had been doing versus an openness towards others and towards new situations. It was a struggle between creativity and rigidity. Very much like the movement of an earthquake, the two opposing plates rumbled, pressed against each other so fiercely that something had to burst forth. That's when I got sick."

"So in this new synthesis you don't have to hold onto something as fragile as a job for your needs."

"No, not entirely anyway. It really was fragile too, though I had not seen it that way last year when I was scrambling to stay on top of things."

I brought Z a bottle of Jesuit wine with the Manresa label

and said: "Since you have been seeing the Jesuits of late, you should be in on one of the Jesuit traditions. That of receiving wine at Christmas."

"Thank you very much. I really appreciate it. Man-ray-sa."

"No. Man-ree-sa, that was where Ignatius had his first retreat experience, a cave in Spain."

"Oh, so that is very appropriate."

December 17. I was still struggling with the rejection of being booted out of office. I knew I should be free, but I was not. I sought satisfaction from having a job, even though this security was transitory, a will o' the wisp.

I had now finished the usual time for recovery from an acute psychosis. It was closing in on January. Looking back, I could see I had made considerable progress during those five or six months. Since I was unemployed with no definite goals, the slack time made me feel worthless. I had no niche, no soft spot to land. I hesitated to direct my energies in any direction since I was so uncertain of the outcome or of my own abilities.

During Christmas vacation Steve and I and four other Jesuits went down to Sandpiper Beach on the Oregon Coast. Raucous waves, turbulent from the roaring wind, rolled in on the beach, and grey, somber clouds danced overhead. Sandpipers darted in the sand, plucking at the grains, sifting for sand flies and then sweeping out in arcing, graceful bows in the gusty wind. As I walked and pondered, I knew my interests were in writing and in spirituality. On New Year's Day the six of us drove to a local bar to watch the Rose Bowl and to sip Bloody Mary's. The zesty, peppery drinks warmed us. Spicy wit laced our conversation and the game lulled us into a soporific whiling away of the hours. My self-doubt and hurt feelings floated away with them.

My security in insecurity did not last. The next week I laboriously wrote out my reflections from the strolls on the beach as once again I strove to decipher the future:

1. Whatever I do I want to get involved in personal relationships with others. I would not be satisfied with a superficial post. Z compared the difference between a Public Health Officer, concerned with programs, and a general practitioner, dealing directly with people.
2. I feel a deep interest in spiritual ministry. This could be in the form of retreats, research on spirituality, theology of psychology and spirituality.
3. I would not be interested in teaching on the high-school level again. I would be too tense and find it too demanding.
4. I have not ruled out high-school administration, but the need for Jesuit principals seems to have passed. Qualified lay people can be found. I do not envision myself in the role of high-school president. My interests lie in the spiritual and academic formation of students and faculty. The president's role seems inevitably to revolve around fund raising, public relations and a certain social breeziness at which I am not adept.
5. In any event I would want to go on for at least one year in theology. I would like to prepare myself more solidly for the work of the Society, which I foresee as revolving more and more round direct pastoral and theological ministries.

In January I was invited to give a retreat to a group of women in Vancouver, B.C. I had plenty of material from my previous six months of reflection and grappling with my own interior. Based on Van Breemen's book, *As Bread that Is Broken,* the first talk dealt with the courage to accept acceptance. I sat at a small wooden table with a dim lamp and spoke to the 30 assembled women, most of whom were older, although a few younger ones brightened up the room. Rather stiffly, I started in:

Faith is about life, my life. It help me to live better, to be more human, to be more integrated. Faith discovers that there is only one source of life, and one unity, God, who is more intimate to me than I am to myself.

The deepest need of the human heart is the need to be appreciated. Every human being wants to be valued. The deepest love is love of acceptance of *who I am.* Every human being craves to be accepted, accepted for what she is. When I am not accepted, then something in me is broken. A baby who is not accepted is ruined at the roots. She will always be grasping for a foundation to build on. A student who is not accepted finds it difficult to learn. A woman at work who is not accepted by her boss or colleagues may develop ulcers or headaches.

Acceptance means that the people with whom I live give me a feeling of self-respect, a feeling that I am worthwhile. Acceptance means that I am welcome to be myself. Acceptance means that though there is a need for growth, I am not forced. I do not have to be the person I am not. My potentialities unfold at their own speed. I am liberated from craven fears. An accepted person is a happy person because she opens up, because she can grow. To accept a person does not mean that I deny her defects, nor gloss over them.

One sign of non-acceptance is guilt. A vague uneasiness that I am responsible for not being accepted occurs. I may think, for instance, that I must not be lovable because my parents did not seem to care for me. So I may cling to things and develop materialism. Or I am frantically involved in activities to fill up the void.

We all have some traces of such symptoms. No human being can give us full acceptance. Our parents, our spouses, and friends try. Only by God am I accepted *as I am,* and not as I should be.

St. Augustine says: "A friend is someone who knows everything about you and still accepts you." This is the dream we all share: That one day I may meet the person to whom I can really talk, who understands me and the words I say—who can listen and even hear what is left unsaid, and then really accept me. God is the fulfillment of this dream. He loves me with my ideals and disappointments.

It takes a long time to believe that I am accepted by God as I am. How often have we been told that it is important that we love God. And this is true. But it is far more important that *God love us!* We measure love. God does not. God can only love totally, 100 percent. Paul Tillich, the theologian, has defined faith as the courage to accept acceptance, and he means acceptance by God. Very often it is courage that is lacking. We have disappointments or are discouraged. We ask, how can God permit this?

God's love is infinite, so we cannot grasp it, narrow it down. All we can do is jump into it. And we do not like to jump. We are afraid to let go. It is fairly easy to believe in God's love for others. But why me? Few people can really accept themselves, accept acceptance. Self-acceptance is an act of faith. When God loves me, I must accept myself as well. I cannot be more demanding than God, can I?

When I finished, several of the women asked me for a copy of my notes, so I felt I had struck a responsive cord even if most of the ideas were lifted from Van Breemen. I did not know if I had the courage to accept the gift of what I had said. I felt hollow. The words were true. They were important. But I could not live them myself.

February 1, 1976. Time drifted on and me with it. The long gray, overcast skies of Portland mirrored my mood and cast a spell of indifference over me even as I strove for a place to land and scrounged my imagination to find a future. I was still undecided about next year, though I had spoken with Jim, the assistant provincial, and with Ken, the provincial, about doctoral studies in the theology of education. Jim suggested a year of theology which would leave open the possibility of a doctorate without actually committing myself to it. Everyone seemed supportive of my ideas. Some wanted Zieverink to crystal ball my future, an anxious bit of buck passing. I wavered back and forth on doctoral studies, still sifting the field. I teeter-tottered between spirituality and education. At Christmas I was convinced that I should pursue spirituality and psychology. Since then I had kept jumping around, unable to land on a solid field.

February-March. I continued to be a jack of all trades. Zieverink was a bit perturbed that I insisted on doing all things well, as if I were an expert on everything any Jesuit was expected to do. I taught a math class at Jesuit High and a religion class at a local girls' high school. Most of the time I piddled around. My energies focused on the plans for next fall. My sessions with Zieverink were at a standstill and I was hamstrung by the lack of opportunities. In early March I gave a nine-day Novena of Grace in Missoula, Montana. I felt adequate. Nothing was soul satisfying. I met some new people who were kind enough to compliment me. I was invited to throw my hat in the ring to be president at Gonzaga Prep, but after some initial excitement with the idea, turned it aside. I was not ready for that type of pressure, and I would have found fund-raising oppressive.

April. Shortly before Easter I wrangled an assignment to work at St. Aloysius parish in Spokane for two months. My sessions with Z did not seem to be headed anywhere. I pressed on him my need to do something significant; finally he agreed that I needed a meaningful job in order to garner a sense of accomplishment. As I wandered around the Jesuit High campus, I knew I would not be returning. I should have felt nostalgic, saddened at leaving, but I did not. The pale purple carpet in the hallway had been replaced by a rainbow-colored one. The administration was drifting on a course which I knew little about, like distant relatives who have children about whom I knew only the names. I was enthusiastic about the job in Spokane. Finally I would have an opportunity to practice spiritual ministry on a full-time basis.

I was uncertain whether I had come to grips with all my problems. However, my thoughts were no longer racing. My days were tranquil, although boring. I had read an article recently on a study about 100 priests who had left the priesthood. Typically they were compulsive, perfectionistic about their work, and craved recognition and approval for their work from superiors. I had a dose of that for sure. Since childhood they performed well from fidelity to household chores to achievement of athletic and academic honors. Each achievement brought approval and satisfaction. But the individual learned to perceive his value from his accomplishments rather than from simply being a person. Perhaps I was avoiding my unconscious because knowing myself involved a painful process of digging through the undesirable hard strata of the past. My psychological progress hit the doldrums so I was eager to move on. I was no longer on medication, so I was assured that I was on the right track. My fears had subsided; my only significant anxiety was that I would get sick again although I knew that one of the main sources of this illness had been the intensity and isolation of the retreat.

I bid farewell to Zieverink. I do not remember what we said. As I walked out of the stucco building, I noticed that the two apple trees had been severely pruned. Huge limbs had been sawed away; the branches looked handless and stark. The surrounding bushes, however, were tinged with a spring red as the stocks emerged. The trees had the yellow-green crown that came with a successful passage through winter. My own spring would be determined by the future in Spokane.

Spokane was emerging from winter. The trees were still dormant and the grass was brown despite the warming air. During Holy Week I organized the Good Friday and Holy Saturday liturgies; then the pastor romped through and changed everything. I thought here was a chance to use my assertiveness training but did not since I was uncertain of my ground. Others on the planning team were upset with the consequent confusion, but we dissipated our frustration by carping among ourselves. I began three or four marriage preparations with young couples and felt secure because of all the resources available in the parish. I baptized a child of an Italian family and spent the afternoon gorging myself on Italian pastries and a mound of food. They were delighted that I could speak Italian with the grandparents. I was beginning to learn the ropes although I knew I was a rookie. The parish adjoined the university campus and a house of studies for young Jesuits, so I was beginning to uncover some dormant friendships, taking walks around the campus with the young Jesuits.

I tried to get plenty of rest, to think through tense situations and to make links with potential friends although I was not particularly close to anyone currently in the city. My habits of reflection were stretched as I faced these new situations and sorted out my feelings and the direction I was headed. Through these careful efforts I was making some progress.

At the end of April I gave the homily at the four Sunday Masses. I prepared thoroughly knowing that a number of my acquaintances would be in the congregation. As the Masses progressed, my performances grew from so-so to excellent. At the fourth mass I received several compliments. I was paying a price, however; I was petrified that I would flub or collapse. I was intimidated as I gazed out at the expectant audience. I had used the theme of "Fearful people vs. Joyful people": We fear authorities. We fear weakness and fear sin and so are discouraged. To this the Lord shouts Shalom, a peace of healing that touches one from head to toe. I have overcome the world. So take courage, fear not, I am with you.

The packed church was attentive, but I was extraordinarily tense. By communion time my neck was so taut that I had severe difficulty making the physical efforts to give communion. My brother Dan had come over from Seattle for the weekend. He, the Jesuit scholastics, and a couple dozen people said how well they had liked the homily. But in the midst of my success, the foundations were crumbling.

The tension in my neck flowed into my head and I had a severe headache. The stress of this occasion triggered other emotions that had been simmering like a cauldron. As the pressure mounted, my anxiety did cartwheels. I started to feel that I was losing control once again. I felt threatened with annihilation and inadequacy. My entire past was ripped open to judgments of others.

By Tuesday night severe apprehension exacerbated the mounting tension. I felt like a bundle of baling wire, contorted, misshapen and tight. That evening I took some Thorazine to slow down my engines and to get back on an even keel. I tossed and turned and could not sleep. The more sleepless I became the more anxious I got. A loud noise from the parking lot outdoors terrified me; some presence was lurking in the shadows. I flipped on a light and then turned it out again.

Oh, Lord, don't let me go through this agony again. I've been through too much. I'll scream to death if I have to face the hospital again. Will it work? Will they catch me this time? What if I lose control? My mind will be gone in the jungle forever, stretching, screaming and scratching itself to oblivion. I'm losing control. What was that noise? Is someone in the room again? I can't go to sleep or the demons will possess me. I can't go on like this.

I jumped out of bed to go for help. When I got up quickly, I fell over onto the floor because my head was so dizzy. I was going crazy again. All my control, even my physical control was gone this time. The pattern was happening all over again. Everything I worked so hard for was lost. My head flushed with panic. I crawled around the room and climbed up into a chair and huddled there with fear. I gasped for air. Then I caught hold of myself. I suddenly remembered that one of the side effects of Thorazine was dizziness, especially if I moved quickly.

Just when the lilacs were starting to bloom. Won't be able to go golfing with Tom tomorrow. Just when that relationship was starting to develop. Zieverink. Call Z at 6:30. Have to go back to Portland, get straightened around. Be back in a few days to finish up here. Now just doze off for a bit and wait for the dawn.

Whenever I dozed off, tensed spasms jerked and woke me.

I feared going to sleep because I would lose control, yet if I did not sleep I would be a basket case. Early in the morning I called Zieverink, woke him out of bed and said I had to see him. He knew I was extremely discouraged. I borrowed money for a ticket and with a heavy heart flew to Portland that morning.

Someone met me at the airport. I did not notice who. Portland was a lot greener than Spokane.

Perhaps I could go out to villa for a few days and rest there. Get back on medication. Stop the engines racing. Like a gull that's just lost its fish, circling round and round. Nowhere to go. Curl up on the beach, wet, smelling feathers and die. Spokane again in a week.

In the early afternoon I parked outside the stucco house. The two butchered apple trees had not bloomed yet. Too much pruning. The new receptionist was efficient, a bit sullen. Zieverink looked concerned and decisive. He asked what happened. "My mind started racing again. The tension was too much to take. I thought I was going to lose control and the Thorazine wasn't doing any good. In fact, it made matters worse."

He said: "I want you to report to the hospital as soon as you pick up your things."

I felt crushed. "Couldn't I go out to our place on the river and spend some time resting there?"

He was final. "No, I want you in the hospital. You need to work out some things in a controlled environment."

Steve drove me over to Providence Medical Center in silence. I slammed the door. He offered to help me with my bag, but I declined and left. I was back to zero, back to where I had started ten months before, perhaps worse. The first few days I holed up in my room. I could not stand the chatter in the day room. All the same complaints about the food and the doctors who never showed up on time. Sterile, steel cages. That's what we were in. Monkeys on experiment. They didn't know if they could train us or not. Throw him a fish and see if the trained seal will clap for it.

Lillian stopped by for a talk, but I was unwilling to listen to anyone. I wanted to crawl into a hole and disappear. She said: "About 75 percent of psychotic patients are readmitted to the hospital at least once after the first hospitalization. At least this time you came under your own power. You were upset and some of your ideas were getting out of control, but you didn't crash like last time." Her words echoed hollowly as she walked down the polished hallway.

If Zieverink knew what he was doing, I wouldn't be here. Going to Spokane was a stupid idea. Set up for failure and a laughing stock. Now I'll never get anyplace. Bedlam. Don't those brats ever turn down their radio. Someone's locked up in the security room again screeching his lungs out like a frustrated gull. Gulled. I was duped. Everything was going fine. Death's dream kingdom. A twilight world in this cactus that I live in. I'm a poor player that struts and frets his hour upon the stage and then is heard no more. I hope Zieverink never shows up.

I looked in the mirror at my dull eyes and wan face. I was at the bottom again, though this time it was worse. The climb out of this pit stretched interminably. The medicine may not work this time. Maybe I am immune to it.

After three days in the dreary hospital, I realized that this posturing was doing me little good. I had better get to work again and get myself out of here. *Sure as hell, no one else is going to do it.* I started my journal again, only this time I worked at observations and impressions. Zieverink said: "It's not your fault that you get sick." *That's a rich one. Of course, it's not. It's you who sent me up to Spokane.* I said: "I don't think I blame myself. I have to stay in the here and now. Thinking about the future makes my head race. The unreal future unnerves me."

Across the hallway Sarabel, a compulsive lady, bruised and

beaten, kept yelling like a baby for her therapist to come. She chanted, "Mary Lou, Mary Lou, Mary Lou." Twenty minutes on end. It drove all of us crazy.

In my journal I started to structure my day and to sort through what had happened in Spokane: 1) the lack of enough to do led to isolation, like the retreat experience; 2) my need to excel and prove myself induced feelings of anxiety and lack of self-worth; 3) my need to prove I was no longer sick to my friends and, in particular, the Jesuits.

The Lord scourges those who draw near to him in order to admonish them.

At the end of the first week I sensed a breakthrough. I was sitting under a sycamore tree outside the hospital. As my mind sifted through some roles, I deliberately imagined myself hearing my own confession. I was really both characters: Pat, the confessor who was compassionate and gentle towards everyone except himself; and Pat, the compulsive, neurotic who failed at everything he sought to excel in. The confessional situation brought tears to my eyes and I found the Lord's forgiveness, a gift of self-acceptance and gentleness. We (confessor and sinner) are I. I am I. I am both confused sinner and gentle confessor—growing, groping as one person towards the Lord.

Lord, you don't take away my fear. You let me grovel in it. But maybe I can surrender it to you instead of repressing it. Then I can feel it and live the pain rather than running away from it. McHugh used to say: "Pat, you're running from the cross." If I surrender, then I'll be free, free to be myself, rather than a dull, dumb, paralyzed man without feeling or humanity. I think mysticism is bunk. All I've seen is pseudo-mysticism, a surrender to the feelings that arise from myself. It's a passive surrender to my own fears and anxieties, to the "devil" within me. My feelings explode from the pressure. The danger is self-idolatry or magic. Magic controls and manipulates God. St. Stephen said: "Lord Jesus, receive my spirit." His stoning to the death was peripheral to his vision of you. St. Thomas saw your appearance as the wounded, crucified Lord: "My Lord and my God." Real mysticism is the acceptance of one's humanity.

I fished around for ideas through my journal: Sexuality and positive regard towards others are interconnected. Loneliness leads to increased sexual tension. It can also motivate one to deepen his or her love towards others. If these sexual feelings are repressed, they will surge out anyway. They will arise through compulsive behavior, snobbery towards others, or aloofness.

I'm sick because I can't come to grips with my compulsions. My interior is all jumbled with the exterior. Paralyzed. Gesture without motion. Shadow without substance. In the second week at the hospital I was still depressed at being in the hospital and resented Zieverink for "making a mistake."

Jim and Steve visited me. An hour after they left, I felt a wild emotion of soaring and plunging thoughts. I thought it was loneliness. Lillian suggested: "You're comparing yourself to them. You're angry that you're tied down in this hospital, and they are off accomplishing something, doing what all good Jesuits do." It made sense. I noticed that the ward had not changed much. The staff was the same. The day room was drab and dreary. Since my bed was next to the staff room, I noticed the pounding of typewriters charting and diagnosing the endless round of the day's emotions. The next day I was still angry, felt rotten and did not know why. Zieverink had locked me up for the weekend and thrown away the key. I was discouraged and helpless, like a whipped puppy.

For comfort I turned to my journal, my only accomplishment and source of productive work: I now see the task ahead of me: 1) express my anger in appropriate and effective ways; 2) adjust my image of myself to a more realistic one. Sounds like a Zieverink prescription. Hospitals are confining places. They make you feel so helpless. All privacy is lost. Come on in, everyone! Pat is sick again. See the sideshow. Everyone who walks in off the street assumes they are doctors with helpful suggestions.

My anger towards Zieverink was similar to my blind fury as a child towards my dad. I recalled Macbeth: "It is a tale told by an idiot, full of sound and fury, signifying nothing." No doubt the concept of original sin is traceable to this fury towards parents. Each child in turn blames his parents. The blame flows backward in time to the first parents who sinned, fell from grace, and forever after bred into their children a fury at being helpless and overwhelmed by the adult world.

A child cannot blame God, though he tries, because that is too frightening. The child then feels naked, helplessly angry toward the world. The child in a second flash of fear realizes that God has nothing to do with it, though God could annihilate him. The fear of annihilation is transferred to parents and friends so that it inhibits any expression of anger, first of all, because it would mean loss of control and then, secondly, would mean loss of love. Beneath these fears lies a primordial fear of death and loneliness. The chain of generative, original sin breaks when a person takes responsibility for what he has done and turns towards the Lord and receives God's forgiving love.

As a priest I was gentle, affable and wounded. As a sinner, I was angry, driven to do things, brusque and short-tempered towards friends and parents who were to blame for it all.

Job felt dumped on like this. Lord, you let it all happen. Job is speechless when you finally come. You never do answer his complaints, but you come in a whirlwind. Here I am again on my dunghill. "Maranatha!" Come, Lord, come! Don't deceive me anymore. Come in your incarnate world. Not in the flashy ideas of my twisted mind. Be real. Be present. No more voices or visions or even hints of them.

We mentally ill are the lepers of the last part of this century, the outcasts. Most other diseases have lost their social stigma. Even leprosy or Hanson's disease, can be effectively treated without isolation from society. Only mentally sick people are contained in a separate unit, isolated from normal sense stimulation. Like leprosy, mental illness casts a spell of loneliness. A spiritual dehydration occurs. The spirit coils round itself but never finds its tail nor finds its image in the mirror. Like a blazoned cross on the forehead, the stigma of mental illness remains for all to see and to turn aside in embarrassment.

Graham Greene describes the rage of a frustrated lieutenant in The Power and Glory. *"He was a mystic, too, and what he had experienced was vacancy—a complete certainty in the existence of a dying, cooling world, of human beings who had evolved from animals for no purpose at all. But he believed against the evidence of his senses in the cold empty ether space." Remember the ether when you had your tonsils out. Cold and mindless. I woke with nausea and the pain of a sliced throat. Greene describes Padre Jose, sitting outside the shack hearing his mistress calling him to bed: "There was never anything to do at all—no daily office, no Masses, no confessions, and it was no good praying any longer at all: a prayer demanded an act and he had no intention of acting."*

I shared the lieutenant's rage at the world, at human weakness, at groping and fumbling around in a disheveled mind. I shared Padre Jose's emptiness, his bottomless inactivity. No one could any longer protect me; I was free and vulnerable. The ebbing of rage came slowly. I needed to surrender my anger to the Lord and accept my fragility. Rage clung to every fiber and seeped through the marrow of my bones; it prevented me from any compassion towards others. If I could accept my humanity, then my affection for others might be unleashed. I was repulsed by the mentally ill in the ward.

May 18, 1976. Zieverink stopped by for a brief chat. He was back to his clinical, rather observant, self again. I said: "The image I have of myself is extremely unrealistic. I have been comparing myself to a good friend of mine who seems to have everything I could hope for. By projecting such an inflated ego, I am bound to frustration when things or events don't fall into my life as they should."

Zieverink said: "You have a lot of talent. You need to tap into your own resources. When you are feeling well, you can do almost anything."

Frustrated and with muted voice I said: "I feel that I have taken a vow of productivity at times. Everything I do has to be geared for something."

"What do you think causes your restlessness?"

"When what I think I should do is different from what I feel I should do, then I am anxious."

A woman on the ward reminded me of a girl from out of town that I knew in high school. Brunette. Pert and cute. All the guys had flocked to her at first, but she still had a boy friend in the town she had come from in Mankato. "Ordina quest'Amore, O tu che m'ami."

Zieverink and I talked about relationships with women since I was growing a little uneasy about my own feelings.

"I feel strained about women that I am attracted to. As if my controls might slip."

"Don't forget the normal personal and social restraints that are operative on both sides."

"Because of my fear of personal relationships, I just run from them. I think I was dependent on my mother's apron strings. My self-identity was whatever I perceived as my mother's ideal for me. The perception probably obscured the reality.

"You know Lillian keeps me pepped up. Today she said, 'We all need people. Only the Statue of Liberty stands alone.' "

Zieverink and I talked over my plans for next year. He urged, and I agreed, that I stay in Portland for another year of treatment. I was not about to risk yet another breakdown or even the severe anxiety of having one. The stakes were too high to change horses in the middle of the stream of consciousness.

Steve picked me up at the hospital. We spent a short time at the school, celebrated Mass and had lunch together. Steve quietly observed with his usual insight: "Isn't it difficult to come back and face all these people?" We went bowling for lack of anything better to do, and later went up to the Rose Gardens where the rhododendrons were fading and the first yellow roses starting to bud. Back on the Ward I found I was angry with myself. I felt discouraged. I had given my very best and that was not enough. I was envious of Steve for his freedom of being able to select attractive choices. He was going to Rome in the fall for a program in theology and spirituality.

May 25, 1976. *God does not protect us from our mistakes. He may turn failure into victory by allowing a graced insight. Last year I sought to solve my problems by doing something rather than becoming someone. Face each emotion as it comes. Detonate the land mines before you blindly step on them.*

May 26, 1976. Zieverink dropped one of his timed explosives today. "Your fantasy of your relationship with your father probably did not fit too well with reality. There is precious little evidence to back up your feelings." *Why don't you grow up kid? Instead of blaming everyone else. A burdensome cloud rose out of me. Plough through this and re-evaluate it. My thoughts are as tight as this chemical strait-jacket that they put you in.*

May 29, 1976. Yesterday Steve and I went out to lunch again after I was finally released from the hospital. I was a little more relaxed, he thought. I slept well with the light on. I still have phobias of blindness and darkness. I trimmed roses at the villa and helped Kevin with the planting. *It'll be a month before I recover. Z hasn't indicated anything yet. "It may be another couple of years of therapy," he said. Perceived rejection. Damned little to support it. I feel as limp as a wet towel.*

June 2, 1976. I was suffering from acute anxiety. No one had an inkling of what I was going through. I felt as anxious as I had when they carted me off to the hospital last July; about the second worst day of my life. Razor blades were grinding up my stomach. Nothing alleviated it. Zieverink said: "Your best hope is for long-term therapy." Sounded grim to me. I have hit bottom again; I hope the remainder will be uphill.

June 6, 1976. Played tennis today. Felt better. Would like to drop stelazine, the new drug. Makes me feel like I am taking off in a glider and hovering over the wind currents.

June 8, 1976. I saw Ken, the provincial, today. He had a good psychotherapeutic sensitivity. He confirmed my staying in Portland and continuing in psychotherapy with Zieverink for another year. He encouraged me to find a spiritual father to sort out my spiritual confusion. He also dispensed me from the annual retreat. He said, kindly: "What you are doing is a very spiritual exercise."

June 9, 1976. Today is my 36th birthday. I have largely recovered from the recent anxiety attacks. I have not made much progress this last year. Growth comes in fits and starts. I cannot chart a clear, linear, upward progress.

Rage bottomed out. A voice mixed with music sounded from afar off and floated away again. My "intolerable shirt of flame" would not be easily removed.

December, 1982

"How about some eggnog, Father Howell?" The new secretary was getting into the Christmas spirit early. "I have a little brandy to go with it."

"Go light on the brandy. I still have a lot of writing to finish this afternoon."

At lunch the small staff that was left around the school to clean up the classrooms and run the office was talking about Santa Claus. Joan said: "Eric, my son, is twelve so, of course, he has long ago given up on Santa Claus. But when he first came home and asked if Santa Claus was real, I said, 'Of course, Eric,' and took down the encyclopedia and read to him about St. Nicholas and how Santa Claus got started. It left him with something."

Jim, the janitor, added: "We all need a bit of fantasy."

I chimed in: "Yeah, like the fantasy that your floors will all be clean yet on the second day of school." They chuckled.

I joined the reminiscing. "I was five-and-a-half when I realized the folks were Santa Claus. I got a present from Santa Claus that I had seen the week before in the drugstore. I still remember the exact spot where I had seen it in the store."

Joan asked: "Did you tell your folks what you knew or did you pretend that Santa still existed?"

"I wasn't that devious then. I'm sure I told them."

Chapter Seven
A FEW FEEBLE STEPS

"Your best hope," Zieverink said, was to continue in therapy. A dreary, aching prospect. I had been dealing with my problems in a superficial way and had not touched the rotted roots. The future seemed lonely and the undertaking monumental.

Here I am back to zero again. What are you teaching me now? I need to be baptized again. By the Spirit who blows where he will. I can't fathom the earthy things of my own sickness and disorder. Heal me in the labyrinth of my mind. Drive out the tangled serpents. Shock me out of my stupor. Dredge up the contents of my psyche, mold and breath again through my soul as you once did when you first touched me.

In the search for creativity I took a course called "I Can't Draw" at the Portland Arts and Crafts center. I scratched through a few assignments with limited success. Halfway through the course, the instructor assigned us to draw two or three pieces of fruit, so I painstakingly drew three apples. My friend Mary saw these lovely creations at the next lesson and exclaimed: "Oh, Pat, your peppers are wonderful!"

"They're apples," I wryly laughed.

In July I flew to Minnesota to visit my parents for a week. The rolling prairie was green, burdened with wavy grain. A languid haze clung to the rim of the lakes. A few blackbirds circled in the thermals bursting from the moist fields; ditches filled with water. Bugs splattered the car as we raced along towards the two-year old home where my parents lived along the lake. A flush of begonias, red and yellow, flanked the entrance to the house. I had a good visit and found it relaxing. After a few days Mother asked me: "Is there anything we can do to help?"

Rather curtly I said: "I'm in the hands of a good psychiatrist so I don't see how you could help." I said it automatically in a defensive mood. I was more interested in piecing together the past than in dealing with the present. I quizzed my parents about the early days of our family to rectify and to fill in the gaps of my memory. I had been working with Zieverink on my personal history. Although this history splicing did not seem to lead to anything, I thought it a good project, something I could do well, and it was satisfying to complete the puzzle. Over a period of time I told Z my story:

I was born June 9, 1940, on a Sunday morning at Tanner's Nursing Home. A Gemini. Our local Jesuit High astrologer smiled sagely six weeks before I had my breakdown: "An eclipse passed through your sun sign this week. A difficult adjustment is ahead of you."

After a few weeks my mother would take me out in a "baby buggy" for a walk along the sidewalks lined with elms and box elders towards uptown for some shopping. According to reports, my dad on these occasions always wanted to know exactly what had been said about me, the usual oohing and ahing about a new baby. Evidently I was doted on by my parents.

Within 15 months my brother Mike was born. Reportedly I was jealous but soon recovered from no longer being the only "number one" son. In December the same year, Grandpa Howell died at 77 from a long illness. He had grown popular in Sheldon during the 20's and 30's when he was Democratic County chairman. In fact, one year he was also elected Republican county chairman on a write-in. In 1936 he had a chance to go to the Democratic national convention, but could not afford it and besides Roosevelt was a shoo-in. When he was County Chairman in the early 30's, Grandpa had tried to have my dad give up his struggle with college and take a well-paying Civil Service job he had lined up. Dad refused, evidently with some heat, and continued to peel potatoes at a restaurant in the winter and weed mustard from the fields in the summer in order to continue his pharmacy degree.

My earliest remembrance is of chewing up a tasty book of matches. I liked the salty taste. Soon after I celebrated a birthday, perhaps my third, I won the peanut hunt by ferreting out the hidden, unshelled peanuts scattered around the porch and yard.

The war was enlarging and my dad was restless to move on. Sometime in 1943 we moved to Duluth, Minnesota, where shipping was booming. I was fascinated by the magic of elevators, though my mother reports that I was initially terrified of them. I stepped into a little room, the doors closed, the doors opened and a new sight appeared—usually Dad in a druggist's white jacket. Mother, Mike and I spent hours at the zoo, feeding the monkeys, watching the elephants and giraffes get hosed down. Another favorite sight overlooked the harbor and a draw bridge through which a variety of ships passed.

Eating all our food at table was a must. On one occasion I refused some carrots and stomped upstairs in a great huff to my bedroom. At the top of the stairs I shouted the worst word I knew, "Ship!" I thought it had something to do with those ships in the harbor. For this obscenity my mouth was washed out with vile-tasting soap.

A street vendor hawked his vegetables and fruit through the neighborhood where we "helped" Mom shop. I was intrigued by answering the phone and Dad's voice was usually on it. One day we were out walking in the rain and I stormed: "If we hadn't sold our car, we wouldn't be all wet." That was my only wartime hardship.

Before long we were moving again. Dad bought his first drugstore in 1944 in Hettinger, western North Dakota, a rowdy new town just approaching 40 years old. We were to live above the drugstore next to a saloon. The folks put up their own nest egg, borrowed the rest from a drug company and bought the store. Mother was amazed to look up and see lines of sheet music for sale—something she could never af-

*ford as a girl. We drank chocolate milkshakes from the foun-
tain until we were stuffed sick of them.*

*Not too long after we arrived I came into the apartment
one day and Mother was in tears. A huge picture of President
Roosevelt was on the front of the newspaper with a banner
headline: "President Dies in Warm Springs."*

*I used to enjoy seeing the postcards and stamps my Uncle
Tom sent Mother from the South Pacific where he was fighting the "Japs." I could never figure out how all the jeeps and
equipment could get across that water. In August that summer I was in front of the drugstore when the news of V-J day
exploded in the town. The war was over. Everybody would be
coming home. Hettinger went berserk with much screaming
and shouting, drinking and hugging.*

*In back of the drugstore was a tiny enclosed yard with a
pair of swings. Mike and I played at swing-jumping contests,
followed by shoe-kicking contests. We would swing as high as
we could, then arch our foot and kick our shoes as far as we
could fling them. One day Mike had a superb kick. His shoe
went sailing through the limbs of the tree, through a narrow
opening in the fence, and crashed through the window of our
car. We sheepishly reported this astonishing success to my
mom.*

*My brother Bill was born in December, 1945. We were all
excited when he and Mom came home for Christmas.*

*The next fall I was to start first grade. Willard Solberg, the
superintendent and a good friend of my folks, had me worried
when he claimed: "You can't start school until you can tie
your own shoe laces." I studiously learned to manipulate the
knots. I started off to school with my pencils, tablets and a
patch over my right eye from a sty which I periodically got.
Dad, ever the caring "doctor," lanced the sties and eased the
pain.*

*I loved school. I had a lot of friends and immediately
started competing with them. I thought Dick and Jane*

*readers were great and bounced along with Baby Sally, Spot
and Puff. "See Dick run! See Jane run. Run, run, run." The
word "yellow" was a real discovery for me—that a printed
word actually described that bright color. I was a great hit at
Halloween when I came to school dressed as a robber. I was
made leader of our gang of bandits after school that day. It
was my first leadership role.*

*Mike and I devoured books and comics. One night I woke
up about three a.m. and said to him, "Let's read." So we
did. When we were found out, we resorted to hiding under
the covers to read by a flashlight.*

*At a slightly earlier age Mike and I were very enterprising in
making money. We would rove the back alleys searching out
pop bottles for which we got a penny each from Dad. Dad became suspicious one day when we brought in a load of clean
bottles. We had simply lifted them from the saloon next
door. We were marched right back to return them. Another
time we went on a foray through the town to gather clothes
pins under the neighbors' lines until one bewildered lady
called my mother who was greatly embarrassed by our enterprising hunt.*

*My instincts for saving money were well ingrained. On the
way home from school I spied a framed picture with the in-
scription "girl of my heart" and a picture of a half-clad
Arabic dancer. I presented this to Mom for her birthday and
proudly proclaimed: "And it didn't even cost anything!" She
did not let on that it was anything other than just great. Later
I found she thought it was hilarious and could hardly contain
her laughter.*

*We went to many football and basketball games with Dad.
In the fall of 1947 I was a ring bearer along with one of my
girlfriends for the Home Coming. I was scared witless that
same night when I saw a black man, the first I recalled seeing,
and one of my friends said: "Watch out for that nigger or
he'll knife you." We were also scared of the gypsies that lived*

next to the reedy area of the lake. We were warned they would kidnap us, but we hardly ever saw them and did not test our luck by going down there.

In the fall we went pheasant hunting. Hunting was always a family outing. After one long sunny afternoon without spotting any game, we sighted an owl on a fence post. Mike and I wanted Dad to shoot it, but he was not keen on it. "I'll shoot it if we don't find anything else and if it's still there when we come back," he said hopefully. After another hour we had not found anything and had circled back to the same post. So Dad caved in and shot it. Word soon leaked out around town that "Howell shot an owl!" and Dad took a fair amount of ribbing from all his friends downtown.

Every Sunday we trooped off to church to hear Fr. Copini, a Dutch priest, give a sermon. A couple times I would stay home to babysit Bill which caused me a scruple, not then but later, because "I had missed Mass on Sunday." Fr. Copini and my dad were good friends. Until the war ended and we could buy a car, he would often stop by our house for a visit or take us all for a Sunday ride. Once he brought by a batch of fish and Mike broke out with a wretched case of hives. Mike could not eat fish or even be around the frying of them, so we resorted to lots of beans, eggs, and vegetables for the Friday abstinence.

I guess I had learned my prayers quickly, but I remember Mike learning the "Our Father" at my father's knees. Mike was not doing well, could not concentrate, nor remember the words and was in tears. Dad was rather heatedly insisting that he learn it before he could leave. I became upset that my good friend Mike was under so much pressure.

I remember coming into the living room one night from my bedroom. My folks were just back from a dance and were having a heated argument. The gist of it, I thought, was Dad did not want Mom dancing with anyone but him. I got upset and wanted to defend Mom, but was hustled off to bed.

In July, 1947, my sister Margaret was born at the Springer Nursing home. Dad woke us up at midnight and excitedly told us we had a baby sister. "Oh, good;" we went right back to sleep.

For Halloween the Solbergs threw a party with apple bobbing and other party games. Halfway through the party there was a tremendous pounding and a shriek at the door and a hideous witch stalked into the room with a covetous cackle. We shrank from her as she shook our hands through an icy rubber glove. Before we jumped too far out of our wits, the garb was shed revealing Mom who was always good for a gag.

Mother did not care that much for Hettinger and its rough spirit. She did not like Dad gambling though he often won. She also hoped for a Catholic school to which to send us kids. When Hettinger celebrated its 40th anniversay, the town fathers were about to send the sheriff off to Canada and throw a real whoopdedoo. Mother was not going to have any of it. She packed up us kids and took us on the train to her folks in Oakes for the duration. When we returned, the celebration was over. Dad had shaved his reddish-black beard, and I was surprised at how much larger his nose was.

It did not seem too long after that that we were selling the store, packing our bags to head out West, and bidding farewell to our school friends. The second graders threw a party for me, and each one chipped in a nickel to present me with a handsome sum. I was impressed with my sockful of nickels. We were headed to Renton, Washington, to live with my dad's brother John and his wife Ruby and three cousins, Johnny, Karen and Cathy. I was given a couple of workbooks, and a reader which I dutifully worked on during the long, circuitous trip through Salt Lake City to Seattle.

We arrived at the Howell Big Soos Ranch, south of Renton, on a clear, crisp sunny day with Mount Rainier hanging like a picture at the end of the 75-acre, lush green pasture. We were to be the upstairs-Howells while my aunt and uncle and three cousins were the downstairs-Howells. This arrangement would last for six months while Dad searched throughout Washington and Oregon for a drugstore to buy. Mother had primed us for several eventualities so that we would be on our best behavior. We were to eat everything. The very first night my aunt Ruby served spinach. Mike gave an agonizing glance to Mother for amnesty, but she firmly nodded to eat away. Mike manfully ate some of the spinach then gagged and finally vomited on the floor. That ended the spinach, and it did temper such maternal commands for the future. More often than not, Mike bore the brunt of these skirmishes from which we both benefited.

Mike and I went to St. Anthony's grade school. Each of us was in a class of 50 to 55 students. The same threatening sister taught both the first and second grade. I hated school, and seemed on the fringe on the playground: I was the cousin from North Dakota. Back at the ranch I would take long meandering walks through the peaceful wooded hills. I poked at the brown mole hills and shook the ferns dripping with dew. I always seemed to be preparing for something that never was to happen. But the waters and the wild lured me into their depths. This habit of wandering in the woods got me into trouble when we went up to Mount Rainier Wilderness Park. I strolled off on one of my customary jaunts, chasing chipmunks and squirrels and half expecting to see a bear. When I returned about two hours later, Mom was in a panic and everyone was out searching for me.

Mom drove all of us to school, usually in the rain. She would lead us off in singing "The ol' Gray Mare, She Ain't What She Used to Be" and a thousand other songs. My cousin Johnny liked Mom. They were both actors and could ham it up together. Johnny "played priest" a good deal, and everyone expected he would grow up and become one.

Before and after school were the best parts of the day. After school Johnny and I would trek off to the post office where a blind man sold newspapers and candy. We would religiously buy a box of Smith Brothers black cough drops and then wait for my uncle, Doctor John, to drive us home.

Johnny, my aunt Ruby and I all made our first communion together that May. Ruby joined the Catholic Church and Grandma Howell, 76, came by train from North Dakota to help us celebrate. Johnny and I both had little white communion suits and someone gave me a silver-beaded rosary.

One evening at Benediction I thought God was right there in the monstrance since a beam of light came right out at me from the sacred vessel.

By June no feasible drugstore had come up for sale, and Frank Dills from Lisbon had offered to sell his drugstore to Dad. So we packed to go home. I was happy to leave. I did not like school and I felt tense and lonely around the ranch, except on my solitary walks. I would miss the farm, the ducks, the geese, the horses, and the fishing for slumbering trout with salmon eggs in the Big Soos creek, and my wandering across a log on a pond surrounded by musky, skunk cabbage and then on up into the fragrant evergreens flanked by apple trees in pink blossom. I would also miss John and Ruby, but I was happy to be on the road again going home. We made a leisurely trip of it, stopping in Yellowstone Park on the way. My one-year-old sister Margaret rode like a trooper. She would stand up in mid-seat and swig down a bottle of milk.

Finally we reached North Dakota. As we drove down the west hill of Lisbon into the wooded Sheyenne River Valley, I hummed a little tune of contentment and relief. In that moment I realized I had been fairly miserable for six months, but thought tomorrow would be much better. We had come home.

Zieverink commented several times on my memory for detail. "Did anything traumatic happen to you in those early years? Anything that stands out as a shock?"

"I don't think so. I was pretty happy until we left Hettinger and went West. The tough times came later, but even then I don't remember anything startling."

Summer sped on rapidly. My anxiety level increased at the prospect of teaching English and math again. Dreams came of bedlam in the classroom, wild uproars, and confrontations with students. I woke up in a sweat, fearing the worst and grinding out the pains linked to the past.

At the Vow Ceremony for young Jesuits at the end of summer, I talked with scores of Jesuits. Most of the conversations were safe and superficial. Mike T. asked me bluntly how I was doing. I preferred his directness to people mousing around as if nothing had happened. My own vow day had been a real letdown. A yellow leaf curled up in an old book. Mass at dawn. A strained celebration with loud laughter. Everything was so private; you had to do it all on your own.

I sensed the same isolation one night when I had dinner at a local convent where I said Mass once a week. On the surface the nuns formed a happy, friendly community, but I sensed a strain at the dining table around which fourteen of us were gathered. Everything revolved around two sisters who dominated the conversation. I competed for attention by observing little ironies and by throwing out a quick quip.

My days were filled with trivia. I slept ten hours a night so I would have less to face each day. My stupor relieved the anxiety. A zombie felt less pain. Z and I had little to say, certainly nothing memorable. He filled out the hour with explanations. I replied without much energy, but with anxiety about the future.

I could not tell Mike T. these things at the Vow Ceremony. It seemed so flat and hopeless. "It's been difficult. The worst part was the hospital. But I think I'm doing all right now."

Z suggested that I keep a diary of my emotions. "Write down the things that strike you. Things you feel deeply. Don't make it a doctoral treatise or a publication. It's just for you.

Use it to sort through how you are feeling about the day."

August 26, 1976. Z gave me a lot of hope today. "You'll be able to separate out the guilt feelings and emptiness from the feelings of satisfaction and achievement. In the past many of these were jumbled together." He was amazed today when I told him about a conversation with my parents this summer. "They were making out their will and wanted to provide an inheritance even if I leave the Society. They want to make certain it goes to me." He gave an extra puff on his pipe. "Isn't that a contradiction with what you've told me about your mother and your vocation."

"I guess it is. I always felt the burden of pleasing her by becoming a priest. The discussion of the will made it clear that it was my life to determine freely."

"Maybe you have filled in a lot of gaps with your own imagination."

"The other emotional part was their provision for my sister Ginny who is 16. They asked Margaret if she and her husband Tom would be her guardian if anything happened to them. Margaret burst out crying when they started talking about it."

September 1, 1976. First day of school. Slept well. Little anxiety. Classes went amazingly well. Just like my second year of teaching when I had anticipated all the problems from the previous year. We went in, got down to business. All very friendly and comfortable. Don't know how much they know about my being sick.

September 16, 1976. Either I have them buffaloed or they are extraordinarily kind. All my fears about discipline problems have ebbed away. All is not only calm, but going well. Talked with Z today. I'm trapped by my compulsions. I listen to a thousand "shoulds." I should be a good teacher. I should be able to preach well. I am so bound by shoulds, I'm suffocating. Felt less tense after exploding a bit. Getting in touch with my deeper "I," with more sacred, more humane feelings so that I am less driven, less fearful.

September 17, 1976. I am accustomed to doing a lot of things, expecting, like a child, that I would then be taken care of. If I only work hard enough, everything will be all right. Talked with Z about my stay in Rome. The system was a bag of anger. The Dean at the Greg was an angry, overburdened man with an almost Messianic need to do it all alone. He did not even have a secretary. Bit of myself in the dean's workaholism. Compulsive drives. No wonder I got into several spats with him. Leaving Portland might break the cycle. I could breathe a new air. Now I'm caught in egocentricity and uselessness.

September 26, 1976. Said Mass at St. Cecilia's Parish today. Marge, a Jesuit High parent, commented: "You really look good. I hope you feel as good as you look." Homily I gave was: "The truth will make you free, but first it will make you miserable." My own medicinal truth needs to be self-administered. Freedom comes gradually.

October 13, 1976. I live day to day. Paralysis. Can't plan for next month, much less next year. No direction. Theology and literature are attractive. But what would I do afterwards? I have the seniors reading *A Portrait of the Artist as a Young Man*. Joyce gives the bleak grayness of growing up, all those pushings and spats on the playground. I felt soiled and depressed by the roughness. Dismal North Dakota winters. Muddy springs that last forever. Tripped and shoved to the mud. Parents angry. Was it at me or at the roughness?

November 14, 1976. Despite the constant rain I felt better. Z thought I looked more relaxed. Better than last spring. Great! Why didn't you tell me then. Less need of control. More accepting. Less need to prove myself. "You still are looking for the perfect existence, free of stress." No emotional nirvana here. It would be nice to have his command of himself. Stuffing a pipe with thoughtful control and balanced insight. Back to the doldrums, that is where I really was. Z outlined a career plan. "What you need to consider in making career plans are: 1) to find an emotional support system, 2) to discover something you enjoy, and 3) to land in something you are competent in doing. I have been very fortunate in having all three of these come together in my own work. It's not the usual thing.''

Dream last night: my dad took a long Arabian sword from me. Intense anger. All these father images are confusing. He chain-smoked cigarettes. Not for me. The dank day-old smell of burned-out cigarettes caused nausea. Dump those ash trays.

December 15, 1976. A modicum of progress and a glimmer of my future. Nothing seems to jell.

February 11, 1977. The trying months of Christmas passed without registering any change. On an even keel and keeping up appearances. Analysis has picked up again after a winter freeze, left out in the cold kneeling before his eminence. Relationship to parents falls into time present and time past of adolescence. Close to my mother during my teens. She depended on me. My father sometimes aloof. Maybe just silent. Seemed angry though. Was he going through the same anxieties I'm going through? He would have been about 45. Lost his teeth then; a little slack-jawed. Time present: Dad is closer. We talk together about politics. I'm no longer intimidated by his silence. It's comfortable and I don't need to fill in the gaps. Mother is constant, still supportive.

Analysis is a tedious, drawn-out process—three times a week since last June. Layer by layer is peeled away. Could take years. Would the onion peeled away have anything left? Resistance keeps me intact. Some survival skills remain, some impede the way.

With the seniors in English class I am taking Hemingway's *A Farewell to Arms.* Fredrick Henry says: ''The world breaks everyone and afterwards many are strong at the broken places. But those that will not break it kills. It kills the very good and the very gentle and the very brave impartially.''

I'm broken and on the mend.

Applied to graduate school at Harvard, Boston College, and the University of Chicago. Great tussling with Jim at the Curia on this assignment. I thought he was trying to play doctor since he insisted that I should not undertake studies because of my health. Resented his intrusion. Brought out my big guns and we had a knock-down, drag-out argument. He's a great debater and rather enjoys it. Respected my integrity and the force of my arguments. The tussle was productive and convincing.

February 12, 1977. *Roots* by Alex Haley was published. TV program based on the book. Perhaps I could do something similar using my mother's letters. Much easier to correct and criticize than it is to create.

Cleaned up the flower bed for the crocuses which will bloom shortly. Yellow-green memory of spring in North Dakota. Had to be April. Mother, Mike and I swept the hillsides of the butte for wild crocuses hiding under the brown, winter grass. As I dug around the crocus bed, I recalled Haley's *Roots* gave a sense of belonging to the black people. Families provide the acceptance and love we need. Successful Jesuits find this support in community life. Some escape through their work and hectic schedules.

March 3, 1977. Dad is 67 today.

Two dreams: I was molding in clay. I created my face that turned into a pink carnation. In the second dream I painted a dark blue, wooden icon of myself. A beautiful picture from every angle. In the center were two male figures. No teacher was instructing me. On a deeper level, beyond the frustrations, I was recreating myself.

Gave an informal retreat at the beach to five juniors and seniors which centered on issues that they were concerned with. In the afternoon the sun pushed through the fog and then scattered it. We played "fooze" ball on the beach for hours. First I was limp and then stiff as a starched shirt from the romp. Back at school I felt a wave of loneliness. I already missed the companionship on the beach. A faint glimmer of joy in a dreary winter.

March 24, 1977. Z's in Hawaii for a week. Recurrence of chest constrictions and lots of tension. No purpose, just drift and ennui. Still casting around for what to do next year. Gave a homily at Lourdes Parish on Jesus as the Peaceful Revolutionary. He identified himself with the poor and the powerless. After Mass a bright-eyed, elderly lady said: "You must be a very good teacher." She added sadly: "I never had such a teacher." Don't think I'm what she was looking for. Rather sad.

March 31, 1977. Saw Z again. "You were anxious because of feelings of loneliness. You were left behind, like someone left in the college dorm during vacation when everyone had left."

I am tired of the whole bag. Frustrated that I cannot do anything.

April 3, 1977. Decided to go to the University of Chicago for a doctorate in education. Seems viable. Somewhat of a disappointment since I wanted to go to Harvard, but they accepted me for only a one-year program. Cannot say I am enthusiastic about the prospect of the city of Chicago, but at least we have a Jesuit theologate there, so the community situation should be workable.

April 8, 1977. Came out of a slight daze in therapy today to hear Z saying: "Your father was a very ethical, critical man. Perhaps, though, your fantasy of what was going on during adolescence doesn't wholly match the reality. It'a great awakening at ages 18 to 21 when one suddenly realizes that not everyone thinks like you do." Z had been talking for a long while. I strained to let it sink in.

"Dad wasn't very keen on telling stories about himself, but he told the story once of his confronting a doctor who was creating morphine addiction among his patients to support his own addiction. Dad told him either to fold his practice and leave town or he would report him to the Narcotics Bureau.''

"The world is not as hard as you think," Z said, "though the perfectionism of your father may have led you to think otherwise.''

May 8, 1977. A year ago I was back in the hospital for the second time. The pits. Despaired for a few days of ever climbing out again. Still do not know how to resolve the tensions that come to me. I am leaving Jesuit High after five years. Also leaving Z. Still have to be perfect and feel the strain of the strictures that bind me. Arranged with Pat, the novice master, to direct my retreat at the end of the month. Hope it is less dramtic than two years ago. Scary to think what might happen. I am adrift without an annual retreat, though, and think I can handle the tensions as they arise.

May 10, 1977. Difficult to think of leaving. Real affection for some students, especially outside the strict, controlled classroom. Only five classes left. "I felt some separation pangs," Z said, "when I left the Sixth Ward. I set up the complex and hired most of the staff two years ago. With my new job as director of all the programs I have to leave this behind.'' Did not realize his position since he rarely talks about himself.

May 12, 1977. "If you were not going to Chicago, I would recommend another year of psychotherapy. There is a lot unresolved that needs restructuring.'' Felt blasted. Ruminated over it. "It would have been so easy for him to have said something—to give me some reassurance." But he could not. He cared for me, but he could not express it. He tried to show it by giving me my independence. Dad would say: "Whatever you do will make us happy.''

May 18, 1977. Back in the old, stucco house, I said: "My relationship with my father went in stages. When I was a kid, he couldn't show affection or support. I figured he was angry with me. Now he is warmer and interested when I talk to him. It's easier to talk with him as an adult.''

"In high school, I felt I didn't belong to anything. Inadequate at home, I felt the same way at school. I excelled in class and studies, but felt like a klutz around many of the kids."

"You still have some of the same feelings when you talk to your parents, and you feel inadequate around other people."

"I can't get hold of these feelings. Psychotherapy is like trying to open a door without a handle, prying your fingers in the crack to pull it toward you."

That weekend I made a Marriage Encounter with a couple from the high school who invited me to join them so that, as a priest, I would have a direct understanding of the program. In the course of the weekend, I had to write a number of letters to our little triad, describing my feelings and attitudes. The first letter was a self-description: "I'm like J. Alfred Prufrock in Eliot's poem. I hesitate, procrastinate to make a decision and get bogged down in trivia. 'We have measured out our lives with coffee spoons.' It is all so trite. I am intelligent, enjoy a stimulating conversation and I am impatient with the banality of some people's conversations and interests.

"I have always been interested in studies, but in the last year I find myself overcome by inertia. I can't stay with any project for more than a brief time. Through prayer I have mellowed so that the harshness of judgments toward myself and others has softened.

"I sometimes feel insecure in teaching or preaching because I am afraid other people will see my weaknesses and think less of me. Somehow I have to be perfect so that my parents, friends and everyone else will approve of me, like in high school when I got straight A's. I still have to get straight A's in everything and I feel jealous of others and sad at my own inferiority."

Later that day I wrote another letter about the atmosphere in our Jesuit community. I picked the subject because it was analogous to a family's love for each member in its mini-community. So I wrote:

"As Chuck (a Jesuit priest) pointed out this morning, we Jesuits were trained to do it alone. On that lonely hilltop at Sheridan, our feelings were suppressed and suspicious. The strong, virtuous man followed the rules which were designed to produce strong minds and weak hearts. I am sure that is why so many Jesuits became mavericks, because a maverick does it alone. He doesn't need the feelings of others and suppresses his own feelings.

"Some of this is changing. I formed some close friendships during my years of training. I suppose that was the case of most Jesuits who survived, despite the system. In an active apostolate these friendships are harder to form because there are more ways of escaping one's need for companionship. I can easily build up my own inviolable baliwick.

"Even community meetings to share feelings and thoughts are threatening to some people. Encounter is a dirty word; personal involvement is suspect. Why not? They have been that way for years.

"Our community is not much different from most—perhaps even a bit better. Lately I have been able to share myself in a slightly more open way. Others are so habituated to escaping their emotional life that it comes now only indirectly or else disguised as anger at some kid or administrator. Suppressed hostility is never directly vented.

"Ignatius frequently said that in our prayer we may discover the Spirit working through us by attending to our feelings, but in our community these feelings are so suppressed or so contaminated by anger that discernment can hardly take place. The Spirit is working, but slowly, very slowly."

In the concluding letter I wrote: "The feeling I find most difficult to express is my anger when I am frustrated and out of sorts. This repression probably goes back to childhood when I was afraid to be angry towards my father; he was so big and awesome. I felt guilty over being angry and so even today I will avoid disagreement at all possible costs. But it acts like a raw wound stung by hornets again and again. Some of my insecurity in teaching class and preaching is traceable to this suppressed anger which crops up in conflicts.''

One of the speakers at the Marriage Encounter quoted Abe Lincoln: ''People are about as happy as they decide that they are going to be.'' Thinking about my own insecurity and plagued by doubts, I shied away from such a decision.

I ended the school year by thanking my two English classes for being so supportive during the past year. I said: ''You all know that I had a breakdown almost two years ago and that I have been struggling to regain my health. One of the things that has helped me the most has been teaching all of you in such a positive, creative atmosphere. I have enjoyed it all. I wish you the very best for your own futures. I hope you have learned as much as I have learned this year and I thank you for all your help.'' They gave me a rousing, standing ovation.

December, 1982

Grandma Howell had a flourishing Christmas cactus on the bureau in the semi-lit dining room, across from the glistening China closet. The delicate flamingo blossoms bloomed two weeks before Christmas. So when I spotted one at a party last week I asked for a cutting for our Jesuit community.

During the vacation break I'll sift through these proposals for next year. The President wants me to stay as principal. The Provincial initiated a discussion about joining his staff, and my interest in theology and psychology keeps surging to the surface. Boston College or Catholic University must have what I'm looking for.

Chapter Eight
FROM OUT OF THE DEPTHS

I returned to the Bavarian-style novitiate at the end of May to make my annual retreat. The old corridors, the worn carpets on the creaking staircases, and the atmosphere of wasted space aroused specters which I hoped had vanquished. Fears of the horror and the black void now swept through the fabric of my being; my neck arched and spine tensed. I was steadied by my urgent desire to make a retreat to prove once again that I was a genuine Jesuit. Yet the specters would not fade into the tarnished woodwork. The air spun with my tortured days in this crumbling building. After rising steadily, patiently for many months, step by step, I now gazed out over a cathedralic precipice into the swirling, cataclysmic vortex below me. Dizziness poured in upon me and the panic of powerlessness weakened whatever resolve remained.

I sat down in a chair in the cramped room where I had flung my battered suitcase. I closed my eyes and talked it over with Z. "Why do you need to make this retreat?"

"I need to face my demons and prove to myself that I can do it, that the retreat wasn't the real cause of my breakdown," I said hesitantly.

"Who's directing or helping on this retreat?"

"I have the best person in the province, Pat O'Leary. He's been the novice director for a year and has great understanding and sensitivity."

Z scanned my visage for quivers of doubt. I stared back at him as long as I could, then dropped my gaze. "All right. Go ahead. But call me if anything happens and take your medication with you." I had weaned myself from stelazine about three months ago.

I need to be vulnerable for anything to happen. God can't

heal me if he can't touch my warped psyche and unleash the demons that drive me. If my prayer becomes more genuine, I can be more alive, more joyous and better understand other people. I need to spew out all the sewage that's been stored up within my aching bowels. A spiritual catharsis. Some kind of shock to the system might finally release my creativity to get on with the building of my life. Didn't the Ancient Mariner have to do penance, tell his story over and over again to be shrived, to wipe away the pang and the curse?

Swift as a swallow in the night I came to my senses. I looked at the cramped room with my disheveled clothes scattered on the bed. The agony was spent. The strange power of inner speech which came from talking with Z restored me. I was sadder and wiser than two years before, but somehow I had to once again make that treacherous voyage out into the deep.

I need to attend to the present, the here and now. I have been healed, but not totally, already, but not yet, as the Gospels say about the coming of the Kingdom.

I settled in, unpacked my suitcase, straightened up the room. They never had enough hooks or hangers in these guest rooms. I looked in the scratched mirror above the sink. My jaw did not sag like it had a year ago and my eyes had a brightness to them. I felt healthy, and arched and flexed my back.

Out of the depths, my soul was uneasy about my relationship with God. My retreat two years before had been so volcanic. *How should I pray? What is God's voice in my life? Am I deceived by the daydreams and voices that come to me? Trust is the foundation of my life. But what rock is there to build on? How can I discern the motions of my soul in its deceptions from the soft urgings of the Spirit? If I monitor myself, at least I can control that much of my prayer.*

I resolved to watch my sleep and dreaming. If I was sleeping well, it was a sure sign that I was getting my rest, attending to my conflicts, and managing my resources. I gave myself permission to do nothing during the retreat. If I did nothing more than survive the week, I would be happy. Of course, I desired much more than that.

The Lord is gentle. He calls me forth to be myself in his love. I come squirming like a stubborn child. I am a servant of the mystery beyond my reach.

Pat welcomed me into the novice director's room, a polished wooden floor, several bookcases, Naugahyde red armchairs. I eased into the chair and watched him flip his wavy, gray hair past his brow. He had a reassuring presence. He did not probe the past, but rather tuned in on how I was doing in the retreat. Responding to my initial dread of this retreat, he suggested a few themes for prayer. "Fear is a noon-day devil that only the Lord can drive out. Isaiah says, 'Do not be afraid, for I have redeemed you. I have called you by your name, you are mine.' Fear shrivels up our love; makes us rigid and unresponsive. Despite all the pain and whatever you have gone through, God is with you and nourishes you, watches over you."

Reassured by Pat, I gained more confidence in myself. I was at peace, rested from a long bout of turmoil. In my sleep, though, I was restless. I argued back and forth with myself and at dawn an echo of the nighttime voices rang in my ears. Nothing remained except the vague uncertainty of confusion.

I gave thanks for the mysteries of the night and the dawn of the day. I ambled along the walkways of the novitiate grounds. The rhododendrons had ceased blooming and a few petunias were gathering strength. Nothing much was happening and I was pleased to be surviving. *At the depths I fear You. I have no control over how you touch me or throw me into turmoil. Your invitations are a threat. If I walk on the stormy waters, you may leave me to flounder in my weakness.* I rested in the security that the Lord would lead me through this matrix of change.

John the Baptist is a wild character. An unlikely hero on

the fringe. How'd he get them out to the desert? Call to repentance and a forgiveness of sin. Blockage. Distance from God. A rupture of the lifeline with God. I need healing badly. Christ heals the relationships between a person and God. He abolishes the Law because it blocks God and cripples people. Tax collectors, prostitutes and sinners stream towards him. Mental cases (possessed by the devil?) are some of his favorites. It's hard to admit I need healing. How about my perfect image? It's all right to be weak. It's all right to be sick. I don't need to feel guilty about it. The Lord traces his gentle finger over the weaknesses and mends them. My fierce competitive motivation remains. Peter was impetuous throughout his life. The scars remain but are stronger in the broken places.

I walked down to the Rose City cemetery. A stone wall closed off the graves from the busy street. The tombstones were a dreary history, such brief reminders of men and women's fraility. Early settlers of the Portland area. Often from New England. Henry Peabody. Born 1856. Died 1930. Really second-generation Oregonian. The pride and prowess of settling a new country were already behind them. They told hero stories about their parents, not themselves. Were the children intimidated by the success of their parents?

I can't acknowledge weakness. Spiritual machismo was the novitiate norm at Sheridan. One had to be perfect! Paul's a better model than Peter for me. Saul's strength was in knowing the Law and rooting out Christians. The Lord changed all that. Paul must have wondered why he went through all that training. Why those years of rule-keeping and perfectionism? I rejected some of the more superficial aspects, but at the depth I was trying to be perfect, not to admit weakness. Just like John's Gospel and the children of Abraham. Until you admit your sinfulness, you cannot recognize Christ. If you're not human, you can't see the human side of God. No person can earn God's love or stand before him boasting of his

*achievements to win his approval. God gives his love freely
and without constraint through Jesus.*

I wandered down to the basement of the novitiate and into
my cramped little room that had been carved out of a classroom along with four other guest rooms. I mused on what I
would do the rest of the summer. Perhaps I could do some
clinical pastoral program at the state mental hospital or back
at Ward Six at Providence Hospital. Mental health could be a
fruitful apostolate. I had the experience and could be em-
pathetic to the patients. I would not be scared off by bizarre
behaviors since I could see where they were coming from. If it
did not work out, I could always take a bed in one of the
places! There should be something like alcoholics anonymous
for mental patients. These thoughts started to gain emotional
momentum. I would capitalize on my experience. I should
show everyone that I had recovered. I had been through the
program, survived and even thrived. Ward Six would be
more attractive than other places since it was familiar. Working with Zieverink would be exciting. Also confusing. I would
probably be looking for his approval. You have got to be
crazy to want to go back to the Ward!

These ideas excited me so much that I found a great difficulty in concentrating. I was preoccupied by the prospect of
finally doing something worthwhile. My spinning ideas raced
around my mind faster than I could track. I had to gain control again of the steering mechanism and gear down. I tried to
put everything related to a summer job or to the mental wards
out of my mind. I listened to a couple of symphonies to calm
my frayed nerves and to concentrate on something outside
myself.

The next morning I woke up aroused from the previous
day. I was relieved I had slept reasonably well, but was still
highly agitated. I had my usual breakfast of Wheaties and
orange juice and nursed a steaming cup of coffee. I focused
on what was going on around about me rather than my own

racing ideas. I strolled outside along the lawns glistening from the dew. *It isn't worth it. There's too much at stake to fool around. I could call it quits in this retreat after six days. I could call Zieverink to see if I could talk with him. All I wanted is a little time with the Lord. I don't need any great lights or spiritual insights. I have had plenty of that.*

A director-type voice said, *"But it is a question of generosity."* A mighty, massive roar of emotion surged up within me. I felt a great violence as I shouted back, I DON'T NEED TO PROVE ANYTHING TO ANYBODY, NOT EVEN TO GOD. Then anger came flooding out in tears. I had been trying to prove something to Pat, the retreat director, and to others too, like Zieverink, my Jesuit community, and most of all to myself. I shook with rage. *You are your own best director and having someone else does not free you of that responsibility. So what direction do you take now?* I wasn't certain yet. I was still shaken by the violence of my own emotions. Jittery and nervous, I kept repeating: "I don't need to prove anything to anybody, not even to God!" I was relieved to gain an insight into the tension I had been experiencing and the root source of it. My need for perfection, for proving myself to others had been ripped at the foundations. This perfectionism was intertwined with my identity as a Jesuit. To question it was threatening since it unwound the fiber of my being. I took a long walk along Sandy Boulevard, gazed on the marigolds, petunias, and flourishing roses along the way. My concentration was nil. Finally I resolved to call Zieverink and to call off the remainder of the retreat. I knew now that there were a hundred ways of *being* with the Lord. Retreats, even prayer, did not have to be one of them. I did not need to prove anything to anybody, not even to God. I knew the truth of it all. This was a foundational moment. I had found a rock on which to build. I had gained my own identity, but the sheer audacity of it unnerved me. I was not only my own retreat director, but I was director, therapist and doctor of my own life. I was in charge like no one else was or could be.

I was disappointed that I could not continue with the retreat as I had envisioned it, but doing things in prayer does not achieve much anyway. I could do nothing and still be loved by the Lord. I shook off my chains of compulsiveness and gazed at them in the gutter.

Since I had not finished the full eight-day retreat, I felt some remorse and a tinge of humiliation. But my anger at such compulsions dispersed whatever sadness still lingered on. Eliot's "East Coker" brought to me the need for beginnings and the ordinary:

> To arrive where you are, to get from where you are not,
> You must go by a way wherein there is no ecstasy.

I did not need anything extraordinary. I needed surefooted realism. I needed to abandon my desires for self-glorification and accept my humanity with all its jagged pain. These disordered emotions whirled and surged around within me like the waves battering an estuary. *I don't need to prove anything to anybody. Be present to your weakness and that's fine. Listen to the music around you and let your emotions flow outward, be healed and disperse. Roll with the waves. Be silent with the silences. And breathe with the wind rather than against it. The bird high up there rolls and turns in the rising wind soars and pushes off on another's power, glides in the stillness, and surges with the sweep of the wind.*

I had given the retreat my best, but I was taught something else. It is God's work, not mine. Being with the Lord is enough. My relationship with God is full of anxiety because I try to placate Him. Fault-finding and sin-offerings are alien to him. It was a God whom I could not trust to be generous and loving. *Delight in finding God by failing to find him.*

When I slipped into the stucco house that afternoon to see

Zieverink, Margot and her mother were not there and a brighter music was playing. Zieverink was pleased when I said: "I was like a ship at high seas in a treacherous storm; I came home to harbor."

"Right. And you had only minor losses. A tattered sail. Namely, you were not able to make the full eight days. How many others making a retreat, do you suppose, experience what you did? Would anyone like to trade positions with you?"

"I suppose not," I murmured.

"Do you have any idea at all how rarely this happens?"

"I don't have much experience with it," I said with a rising courage. "But I think I am my own best director and when I am my own best doctor I will be fine."

"When you are director, doctor, and parent to yourself you will be well." We reviewed a few other things. Then he said, "You have been crazy so you know what it means even better than I. I listen and observe a lot, but it is not the same. Like a child who gets burnt on the stove. It is different from telling it. Thank you for stopping by. I am very pleased with the way things worked out."

I still had a few loose ends to wrap up with Pat, the director. I could see I had been performing in some way for him too. My own compulsiveness was more obvious, because Pat himself was kind, prayerful and flexible. He suggested that I stay around the novitiate in a prayerful atmosphere without regular times for prayer or attempting to make the normal retreat. "No," I said, "I'm done. It's over with. I would be looking for ways to cut corners to get involved again." I was startled by my assertive, new-found courage.

To confirm my direction, he said: "Jesuit identity is not just a retreat. It is centered on a whole range of experience. It embraces the Kingdom and the work of Christ in all its many dimensions."

"Bob and I are going out to the beach tomorrow for a little

break to unwind a bit more. It will be a welcome respite."

"I think that's a great idea," Pat said. "You've had more than enough of a retreat to recharge you."

A vision of childhood, stretching out for a world more full of weeping than I could understand. A flash to the ranch of John and Ruby's, lying before Mt. Ranier. A flower box o'erturned, the brown moles in fresh mounds, the lowing of calves on the warm green pasture and the ferns that dropped tears along the waters and the wild. I had found the child once again and yet he had grown wiser in his loss.

December, 1982

Margaret's Christmas card arrived today. She wrote a clever diary-synopsis of the events of the year. They live in Drayton, North Dakota, one of the world's sugar beet centers. Her husband Tom works for American Crystal Company.

February. *Tom and Margaret keep busy in the winter by curling, an ice sport, and reaffirm that curlers are great people. They also made a few competitors quite happy.*

March. *Tom started his second year with American Crystal Sugar and is fighting the battle of the bulge now that he has a desk job.*

May. *Margaret graduates (finally) from the University of North Dakota with an M.S. in physical education. Sister Ginny also graduates in nursing from U.N.D.*

June. *Margaret looks peaked and tired and feels sickly. A rabbit posthumously confirms suspicions. . . . Due Feb. 18, 1983.*

July. *Swimming pool keeps Jeanine, Jennifer and Joe busy and away from grumpy mother. Wilma, cat of eight years of our affection, calls it quits and leaves.*

August. *Jeanine, Jennifer and Margaret along with Aunt Mel and Grandma Howell go "tubing" on the Ottertail River. Mel, 69, was the best navigator over the rocks, boasting the lightest derriere. U.N.D. hires Margaret to teach aerobics and weight control. Students are informed early that some weight conditions are beyond control.*

September. *Joe, 5, started kindergarten. Awarded "Best Rester" three times in two weeks. He must have adjusted as no further awards are conferred.*

October. *Sugar beet harvest is in full swing. Tom draws the 8 p.m. to 8 a.m. shift. Kids think that Dad's career apes Rip Van Winkle. Jeanine, 10, with some new specs can see the blackboard and learns her nose is not a bookmark.*

November. *Tom, his brothers and Grandpa Zidon bag three*

deer and bring home the meat for the winter as well as enough stories to carry them through until the next season. Howells at Floyd Lake host the Thanksgiving feast. No turkey, no pumpkin pie, and no complaints from a grateful non-chef.

December. *St. Nicholas visited December 6. Must be a shortage of coal this year. Hearing from friends and relatives are events that make December a month like no other and a fitting way to gift wrap the entire year. We would like to wish everyone the very best of health and happiness and God's blessings during this holy time and for 1983.*

The Zidons

Chapter Nine
A RETURN TO NORMALCY

Bob and I drove out to Cannon Beach on a blustery day that promised to get better but never did. I mentioned to him my key experience of the retreat: "I Don't Have to Prove Anything to Anybody . . . . " It lost its impact in the retelling and soon we drifted off to enjoying the day. I did not want to start proving I was all well simply because I had survived the major portion of a retreat. As we walked down the beach and chatted about how the last year had gone, I felt relieved. Bob was a big support by his gentle presence. He knew the pain I had been through better than most. His acceptance sank into me as we trod along the cool wet sand.

The next day I saw Zieverink on one of my regularly scheduled visits. After he had lit his pipe and settled back into his easy chair, he commented: "About half the people in the world have a problem, but don't know it; the other half know they have a problem, but don't do anything about it." He was in one of his philosophical moods which meant he was clicking along on my wave length, rather than the clinical, rather theoretical, paths he sometimes charted.

"I was afraid I would have to go back to the hospital."

"No, I wouldn't do that. I wouldn't punish you." I guess he thought of my hospitalization as a punishment for messing up. I had not thought of it that way, but I could see the logic of it. He was used to dealing with angry people who projected their parental conflicts.

He added: "You can be angry without anyone's permission."

"For three days I have felt euphoric, racing ideas and insights. The euphoria makes me anxious and each new insight increases the anxiety. What really stirred me up was all the anger at God and everyone else."

"I would suggest that the reason you came to see me Friday was to have permission to be angry."

"I was just looking for a safe harbor after being tossed in the tempest. A lot of images from the retreat of two years recurred. I don't seem to be through with them. I get agitated and confused. In many ways the anxiety level is the same as when I was first hospitalized, but my reactions to it are entirely different."

A couple days later I felt recovered. The anxiety had dissipated. I told Pat at Jesuit High: "This retreat was a very healing experience for me. I feel, though, that I came close to going overboard."

"Several of us were worried about how you would do. Some thought the retreat was a poor idea."

"Oh, I didn't know they were concerned. Anyway I can handle more anxiety now than I could two years ago. The excitement of racing ideas is gone, and I don't panic as much."

Just because I was feeling better did not mean that my sessions with Zieverink were closing down. If anything, they became more intense. When I saw him two days later, he said: "You are doing terrific. You're really doing well. I hesitate to say this, though, since you know you don't have to be."

I recalled my mother's saying to me: "You're feeling great, and you look great." It felt more like a command than an affirmation.

"I had a lot of anxiety over the weekend. I think it comes from expressing my anger and then, in the next step, I am fearful of the anger. I want to run from it."

"Perhaps you are also fearful that it will get out of hand and you will lose control."

"I think I am ambivalent about any strong emotion."

There was a pause and then he mused, "You are still ambivalent about your anger towards me. About my letting you go to Spokane, about going to Chicago, and about leaving the hospital."

"I don't think I was that angry with you. I mean you did what you thought was right."

"That may be, but that doesn't change your feelings about it."

I do not recall the outcome of that conversation. I was uncomfortable with the tack it was taking. I drifted off to the ill-fated trip to Spokane. *If I had just been prepared, I could have managed that six weeks in the parish and come back with one success under my belt. Things were just starting to break open. Tom and I were going golfing the next day. I was going to see Paul to start sorting out a few ideas. And the pastor had asked me to preach at the Mother's Day Masses.*

Zieverink was closing in on something. "It is no longer necessary that your father cares for you in a certain way. He can't respond at that level, but that doesn't equate with not loving you. If anything, his love has probably deepened because you can now respond on a different level yourself." *What was the point? What did this have to do with my blowing my chance in Spokane? Nothing was ever going to change.*

I looked forward to my sessions with Zieverink. After the usual introductions, he drew his pipe and said: "I know you better than I know myself. That's the nature of it." His confidence poured over me. Since he said it, I supposed it was true. *If this all goes well, I can find out about myself in depth next year when I go to Chicago. I'll be living in a theologate and taking courses at the University of Chicago. It will be a great opportunity to integrate my psychological and theological insights with my work in education.*

I was startled when he said: "You don't have to be smarter than I am."

"How did you know I was doing that?" We talked about my competitive spirit.

"It is easier to analyze than to be analyzed. Just like giving a retreat is a lot easier than making one. Giving one is like duck soup for you." We slipped back to my own retreat and its tentative resolution. "How many retreatants do you suppose come in and say I AM ANGRY AT GOD and then resolve it. Very few I would suspect. No, I think you made a hell of a retreat."

"It's true that giving retreats, like I'm doing this week with the sisters at Marylhurst, is a relaxing situation. I find it rewarding because I listen to the person directed and I learn about myself. I was giving a homily at the retreat yesterday about the possibility of life after death. If there is such a life, then we have a high degree of personal responsibility. Many feel unequal to this because to accept it would require a transformation of their outlook on life."

"How well are those ideas accepted by your retreatants?"

"Well, on the surface they seem enthusiastic about how the retreat is going. In the individual sessions some of their personal difficulties emerge, but there is little chance to deal with them effectively. I mean we have about eight days. You and I have been at this for two years."

I had not forgotten my journal although my entries were less frequent.

June 15, 1977. There are three main methods by which the cure of a neurotic state may take place: 1) By an analysis of the subconscious of the patient which enables the patient to make contact with the autonomous regions of his or her being; 2) by love given to another human being which lifts one out of isolation; and 3) by a quickening of inner religious life.

The retreat at Marylhurst went well. At first I felt the retreatants were somewhat superficial compared to what I had gone through. I learned to be less harsh as their lives unfolded. The Lord was working through them in surer, less dramatic ways.

June 16, 1977. I am fearful about leaving Z's care. If I have another episode like the Spokane crisis, it may take me a month to recoup again. The retreat at Marylhurst finished this week. I closed with a passage from Micah that I have used many times with myself:

> What is good has been explained to you, man;
> this is what Yahweh asks of you:
> only this, to act justly,
> to love tenderly
> and to walk humbly with your God.

Whenever I read this I thought of Bob since he was the first to suggest it to me in a retreat. He embodied the spirit of Micah: the humble, loving man.

I settled in again at Jesuit High, knowing that I had little planned for the summer but somehow more comfortable with this lack of structure than normally I would have been. *Paul prayed as I would like to be able to. It is concrete. Mysticism is too rarefied, a phenomenon which occurs on the way to probing the outer limits of self, on the way to responding to God's loving call and gift of Himself.*

June, 1977. Father's Day. There was an excellent program on TV, "I Never Sang for my Father." The son battled with his father, but eventually came to an understanding love for the crusty, stubborn man who was his father. I am unraveling the tangle of relationships with my parents. Perhaps only when we are parents ourselves can we understand our own parents and grow to love them as they are, rather than as we fantasize them. Our parental psychic images die, so that we can accept our parents for who they are. Then we are free enough no longer to blame them for our own pains as we did as a child.

June 24, 1977. I flew to Berkeley, California, for a Jesuit workshop on the Moral Development of the Adolescent. The flight down over the Cascade range was immensely satisfying. Felt a tremendous release of energy when I renewed old acquaintances of Jesuits I had met at Georgetown, Tampa, San Jose and other national meetings. I was back in the Society at a vital, vibrant level. I have been released from prison after a long interment. Time is too short to savor everything.

At the second session today, Don Gelpi said: "Sharing is an expressing of faith and is the source for building community. The sign of authenticity in a community is mutual forgiveness." How can I break out of my childish reactions, quit blaming others, and assume responsibility for my own life? Seek forgiveness for my own blindness.

I had first met Gelpi eight years ago in Rhode Island when I was on my way to Rome to study theology. I went down to the beach to visit George who was working on an article. About eight Jesuits were spending a creative summer in an old beach house. One was writing music for the harpsichord. Most of the others were writing books or articles. During the evening social hour Gelpi invited us to cast lots to read our personal fortune through the *I Ching*. He was the interpreter and seer. I cast the "travelers' fortune" which he thought was propitious and then using the Chinese formularies, he cautioned: "Prisons should not become permanent resting places." He thought this sage, Oriental aphorism was most appropriate for someone traveling to Rome.

One evening four of us walked down the Berkeley streets to an Italian restaurant. A religion teacher from Cleveland and I engaged in steady conversation. Later he gave me a copy of Ignace Lepp's *Ways of Friendship* as a token of our own fresh-sprung friendship. Lepp describes a mental exercise which I found helpful. Picture a good friend. Then slowly ask yourself: What do you admire most in him? Next, think through it again and seek to love yourself in him. Finally you might come to realize that Christ loves us because he is reflected in us, just as we love him.

Today is the third day of the workshop. I am feeling

jangled. All the excitement and encounter with new and old friends has stirred up emotions and insights that I have a hard time sorting out.

Today I had an intense conversation with an East Coast Jesuit who had worked at a mental hospital during theology. I talked about my own acute psychosis two years ago, what it meant, how it came about, and where I was now. He listened intently and with understanding. He related his own depression which had delayed his ordination. After I told my story in some detail, he said: "You really know what resurrection means! Because, after all, you went through a death and are now alive." I think he is the first one outside of Zieverink to whom I have related how I felt about the breakdown.

The last day of our workshop. I was surprised to learn this morning that someone I knew was a recovered alcoholic. He has been appointed principal of a high school. Ed said: "I would place much more confidence in such a man." Bill, who was walking with us, said: "Yes, it seems like you have to hit bottom to recover, mellow, and grow."

July 1, 1977. Took the bus to Salinas, California, to visit John and Ruby, my aunt and uncle, who moved there 16 years ago from the ranch south of Seattle. Great nostalgic trip and a break from Jesuit circles. They were as warm and welcoming as I remembered them. Ruby swam every day at the local high school. John, now the urbanized farmer, was replanting large sections of his lawn. Worked up a sweat like a hired hand. The house was filled with antique glassware, cruets, salt shakers, crystal—anything made of glass which they had collected in the last ten years. We toured John Steinbeck's birthplace, saw the original Cannery Row, the Chinese shop and Doc's place. Monterey and Carmel were beautiful. Weathered, ocean-blown Monterey pines and white sand stretches. John's habits remind me of Dad's. The quizzical look of "what now?" Eyebrows slightly arched and eyes wide open. Frequent clearing of the throat and a quiet chuckle over a good story. John thought the world of Ruby, much as Dad did of Mother.

After three days I bused to San Francisco and flew back to Portland. A number of Jesuits suggested that I apply for president of Jesuit High, some of it was serious, some bantering, I thought. Even if I were not going to graduate studies, there were plenty of reasons for my not falling into this trap.

Dave said to me today: "You could come in as president and finish what you started."

I hear an angel saying to me every night in my dreams: "You will be in Chicago next year." I thought of Odysseus tied to the mast by his mates and his ears plugged so that he would not be lured to disaster by the Sirens.

After a break of three weeks from my psychotherapy sessions, I looked forward to seeing Z again. Without a pause I raced through the previous three weeks. It took me about 40 minutes to summarize it all.

"You look terrific."

"I've been listening a lot to other people, so it's a pleasure to talk to someone again who listens with his full attention."

In my next session with Z, I brought up the subject of appropriate expression of male friendship. Now that I had resolved some of the problems of personal identity, other areas which needed integration, such as intimacy and friendship, were arising. In the novitiate the only solution offered for feelings of intimacy, sexuality, or close friendship had been avoidance. At the end of our session, Z gave me a stack of medical journals on human sexuality to acquaint me with the clinical field. From our conversation he must have pegged me for an ingenue. "You'll find these rather egalitarian, that is, probably not in line with the church's or your own position, but wrestling with them may help to formulate and integrate your own thinking."

I spent a couple of hours reading them; the stimulation left me tense. This clinical approach to sexuality did not offer much in the way of integral sexuality, nor did it seem to fit in with my experiences of intimacy or friendship. It was all rather mechanical. After a fair amount of reading, I developed a less erotic and more septic atittude towards these manuals.

July 8, 1977. One of the priests of the community fusses about little projects and concerns in the community. When he returned from his Eastern junket this summer, he started worrying over the new ice machine which was producing ice cubes like rabbits—400 a day. Several of us kept ribbing him about its capacity and offered helpful hints.

"We could use them for ice sculptures or a daily party for 200 guests."

"You could supply us on the hour with frozen daiquiris."

July 9, 1977. Z was in a philosophical mood again. "Affectivity and ending our sessions are related. How do you say goodbye and still maintain at least a part of that relationship. We have only a month to work that out, but I think it is very important." In a different vein he asked: "Does the topic of homosexuality frighten you?"

"I suppose it makes me anxious since it is one of those deeper identity questions, but it is probably no more threatening than many of the other topics we have handled. After all I have been through, I feel I can handle anything here in our sessions. I think homosexuality has connotations which don't jibe with my own reality; I would rather speak of appropriate male friendship."

July 10, 1977. We took up where we had left off. "Was this question of affectivity related to your anxiety while at Berkeley?"

"No, I think the anxiety there was mainly the problem of performance and self-acceptance." Maybe I dismissed this connection too glibly. Self-acceptance and the expression of affectivity seem closely related. Today we covered a range of material on sex, homosexuality, sexual arousal, intimacy and affection.

"I feel as inarticulate now as I was a year and a half ago on other topics."

I was melancholic thinking about finishing with Z. We had about 12 times left. One of these days I have to get up to Ward Six to see Lillian, my shrewd psychiatric nurse.

Had dinner with an old friend. Had a pleasant evening, but at one point he said: "It would be good if you finished the doctorate that you are starting this fall because then people would say you could stand up to the pressure of graduate studies."

What a crock that was. I told him I rejected that compulsive approach to health. "It's a trap of the Society that you have to prove yourself to everyone."

July 12, 1977. Talked about dependency on others and assuming responsibility with Z. I claimed "we" made a mistake when I went to Spokane, but he answered my implied resentment. "You need to take responsibility for your own actions. It was a calculated risk. In addition, the end result of your going to Spokane was better because it turned up new material which allowed me to reassess the situation. You are in a much better, healthier position now than you were 14 months ago when you went to Spokane. I doubt very much if that would have happened if you had kept on the same course you were in here in Portland."

I grudgingly admitted this.

"The trouble with you Jesuits is that excellence is the norm, so you can't appreciate something that is simply good."

It reminded me of a quip from Somerset Maugham: "Only the mediocre man is always at his best." I observed: "We Jesuits are ingrained with the *magis,* the greater good. In straining for it, we neglect our limitations."

July 14, 1977. To close out our sessions, I talked to Z about what psychotherapy had meant to me and what he, as a friend, had helped supply: a counselor-friend, intellectual companion, and a social companion. Of course, we had never socialized. I said: "A friend understands you. There is verbal rapport. I can say things at any level and you understand me. You anticipate what I want to say and appreciate it even when I sputter."

July 19, 1977. Two years ago today I landed in Ward Six at Providence Hospital. These two years have been more *real* than anything I experienced before. Z and I talked at length about the "good little boy" syndrome, how I avoided my father so I would not be punished the way Mike was and about my close relationship with my mother. I felt a strain in my family from the time I was about 8 until I was 15 or so. *I would never have been psychotic if I hadn't made that retreat. I don't think Z recognizes that. As soon as I bring it up he seems to avoid it. He's into chemistry.* "All these stresses and conflicts were there many years before, but somehow when you hit 35, things changed. The chemistry may have shifted. We still do not know enough about the brain and the body's chemical makeup to say exactly what occurred."

Since my personal history had been clarified in our talks, I regularly jotted down my recollections and the newly discovered nuances arising from my sessions with Zieverink. Z focused more on the hurts rather than the data. My view of my own history was more important than the actual history which would need to be recounted in a different way. My sister Margaret could compile the balanced, unvarnished family story. My conversations with Z were about painful childhood memories. I needed to let go of blaming others for my pain and take responsibility for my own life. From my recollections I pieced together a picture of my later childhood for Z:

When we returned from Seattle to the Midwest in 1948, we moved into an apartment in Lisbon, in the house which we would eventually buy, remodel and live in for many years.

Lisbon, a farming town of 2000, was nestled in along the muddy Sheyenne River which meandered through town. A block from the river was our house, across the alley from the Catholic grade school and a block from the Catholic Church. The Kelshes, our Catholic neighbors, lived next to the school. We prided ourselves that we could leave the house at 8:55 a.m. when the bell rang and still make it to class in ample time. Mike thought we should live where Kelshes did so that we could shave off a minute in the dash to class.

I loved my young third-grade teacher, Sr. Margaret Rose. She would mesmerize us with stories which she read right after lunch. The sleepy time of day. The third, fourth and fifth grades were all in one classroom with about 10 to 12 students in each grade. I learned by absorption from the upper classes. I sat behind Sharon Sullivan whom I liked a good deal. Evidently I kept fiddling with her hair on the desk in front of me because one day she whirled around and wholloped me with an open-handed slap. I was more embarrassed than hurt. I told Zieverink: "It was my first defeat at the hand of a woman."

Sometime in the third grade, big-hearted, joyful Sr. James dropped into our classroom after school with a surprise for my friend Jim and me. She laid out a cassock and surplice and asked us how we would like to be altar boys. Apparently it was a real honor although at the time I had not given a thought to being an altar boy. The parish priest Father Al O'Donoghue seemed ancient, but was only into the 20th year of his 40 years as pastor of St. Aloysius Church. He was gruff, friendly, and we were often the target of his Irish wit. Periodically he would sail home to Holy Ireland—it was one word—and bring back gifts for his altar boys, such as an Irish horn rosary. He visited the Catholic grade school to hand out report cards. When I was in the fourth grade, he called me up to his desk, handed me my report card, then patted me on the head and said: "Paddy, you have a head with the shape of a priest."

A year later in 1949 Sr. Margaret Rose left. Shrewish, unpredictable Sr. Gertrude arrived. To practice penance we would have to hold out our palm to have it swatted by her ruler. This touch of asceticism happened rarely, but kept us on edge. She had a fascination for the predictions of Fatima and for the world ending shortly. We were choked by her devotions those two years. I grew to dislike school again. In bed I cried for Sr. Margaret Rose to return.

Since I was passive and did well in school, I became a target of the boys for playground taunts and scuffles. These lasted for three miserable years. One day I was pushed down into the mud and soiled my shirt and cords. I trudged home crying. Mom and Dad laughed it off and sent me back fresh to school. The next day I was shoved into the mud again by someone else, only it seemed more accidental this time. I merrily skipped on home to change once again. But this time the folks were angry that I had allowed myself to get muddied again. I was miserable and refused to go back to school. So Dad said, "In that case you can work," and I spent a doleful afternoon dusting shelves at the drugstore.

I dreamt during these days of sullied scuffles and unhappiness. I was being pursued either by a monster or a gang of ruffians or about to be shot. The enemy lurked underground too as my train sped by in the darkness. One wrong step could mean a mishap. Speed and direction were all important. When pursued in my dreams, I had the uncanny ability to flap my arms and sail off into the sky. At times I hovered 20 feet off the ground and struggled to stay above the fray; at other times I could swing off and soar away from it all.

Another recurring dream was of finding hoards of treasure in mole hills or rabbit burrows—mounds and mounds of precious jewels were in these wonderful treasure troves. I dreamed then of being immensely wealthy so that I could give

*my parents the gifts they deserved. My favorite fantasy was
to use my new-found wealth to landscape the back yard with
lawn, petunias, delphinium, peonies, and manicured bushes.
Although our front yard was well-kept, the back of the house
had been filled in with gravel to cover the mud and a large
trench. With some mix of regret and joy, nine years later I
saw the back yard leveled, scraped, filled with new soil, sod,
bushes and fruit trees. My dream had come true, but it was
not because of my treasure trove.*

*Faced with the brutality of the playground, I preferred to
avoid the taunts. I would rather have stayed in the classroom
and read. This dilemma lasted until the sixth grade when
three classmates jumped me, wrestled me to the ground and
started to punch me. I lashed back, socked one in the nose,
scratched another, and ripped the shirt off the third one. I
was mad, tremulous and nauseous with fear. Actually it was
the last time I recall being picked on. From that point on they
figured I was not worth the cost. Not until a year later did I
notice this taunting was no longer occurring. I was relieved to
gain this truce.*

*Dick, who lived by the river, Jim, my brother Mike and I
were inseparable friends. We took up golf on the sand greens
and dry fairways at the Bissell nine-hole golf courses. We
were there every day but Ladies' Day, and then we would
often sneak in early for a round of nine. We spent long hours
playing croquet, shooting baskets, playing card games and
Monopoly. Mike was the best at golf and croquet and our
competition occasionally caused spats, but they were minor
and soon behind us.*

*On November 11, 1949, my brother Tom was born. Shortly
after, Mother had an infection and was frequently seeing the
doctor in the neighboring town. A mystery surrounded the
illness; it was a tense time around the house. Besides that,
business at the drugstore was much less than Dad had expected when he bought the store. We were scraping harder to*

make ends meet. *The flush income days of Hettinger were over. The household essentials were harder to come by and Dad resented his coming back to Lisbon.*

I absorbed this tone in the shadows and pieced it together more by feelings rather than any direct words. I absorbed, I listened, and I feared the unknown. I loved to listen to the adult conversation. I would sit on the fringe and listen to Dad talk with his older brother Clint about how the New Dealers were selling out the country. Eisenhower had just rescued the country from the dangers of socialism, although at heart he was not much better than the rest of the rascals. Still big government. When I tired of politics and business, I would go to the kitchen to listen to my aunts' chatter. I found it all very engrossing and loved to have company come. I would pump my Grandmother Howell and Aunt Dora for stories about the old days. Then in my mind I would run over them again and again, like fingering a family tapestry.

In 1950 Dad and Mother were invited as delegates to the National Druggists convention in Los Angeles. They asked Grandpa and Grandma Mikkelson to join them on a five-week trip through the West in October. After the fourth week of their absence, I felt an acute loneliness and came down with a severe bout of asthma. The couple babysitting us took fright and the doctor hospitalized me in St. John's Hospital in Fargo, seventy miles away. Halfway to the hospital my asthma cleared up because of all the fuss and attention, but I huddled down in the back seat of the car as if I were still suffering severely since by then I did not dare mention I was all right. It was the only time until 1975 that I was hospitalized. About two months before the asthma attack I had swallowed a dime so the doctors concentrated on that.

Shortly, Mom and Dad arrived at the hospital loaded with trinkets from Knots Berry Farm, shells from the ocean, and a box of Viewmaster slides of the West Coast. In the hospital I felt like a king to be the center of so much attention and was only slightly embarrassed to be there. Soon I was out and back to the dreaded fifth grade again.

That following year my brother Joe was born in October. The folks decided that one of the boys should be named after my father. There were now six of us. Before Joe was born our bedrooms were shifted around, and I was upset by the additional crowding. So Mother took me aside and explained she was pregnant again; the new baby would need room. I was relieved and pleased. We always looked forward to another brother or sister.

School brightened when Sr. Germaine arrived in Lisbon to teach the sixth and seventh grade. Her eyes flashed and her ruddy face flushed with the excitement of teaching or directing a play. When the Irish pastor celebrated his 25th Jubilee as a priest, she produced a play about St. Patrick's arrival in Ireland. With my name I had the inside shot, so I got the lead; my brother Mike was my shepherd companion. Mother was proud of us, especially since she herself had done so much acting in high school, loved skits, drama and the old movies. "At Oakes we had two competing drama groups. The Bison and the Flickertails. We picked up acting from my dad; he was always telling a yarn."

In addition to my dramatic success, my playground troubles were behind me. Though I did not feel secure with my peers, at least I was not their victim.

Sometime in the early fifties, my dad had all but four of his pyorrhea-ridden teeth pulled out. His jaw sagged and so did his spirits. All of a sudden he seemed older. I noticed how gray his hair was getting. I felt a distance or barrier between us that was inexplicable. He was not the same person who had tossed me up in the air when he came home from work or wrestled with us on the living room floor. I tried to talk to him at the drugstore, but I did not know what to say. I knew he had a lot more to say than he did because I had seen how animated he could be when relatives came to visit. Mother en-

couraged me to go down to the store, pick up a few things, and come home with Dad from work. Somehow it did not click. I went out of a sense that things might improve and to keep my mother happy.

The occasional fights between my parents disturbed me the most. One such fight centered on my dad insisting that Mother have a cleaning lady hired to help around the house. Mother thought we could not afford it, and she found it annoying to work with inefficient help. Another upsetting quarrel centered around me. I was washing the dishes. My dad, who was rarely sick, was laid low with the flu. He came out to the kitchen and threw a cabbage at me. I was frightened and went screaming to Mother. A big row ensued between them. I skedaddled outside to get away from the fray, but I was fearful these spats would explode out of control; responsibility for it all shadowed over me.

My brother Dan was born April 2, 1953, when I was in the seventh grade. Mother used to say she kept track of what happened and which year it was by calculating which child was born that year.

About this time my folks began square dancing. Dad, who had never liked dancing that much, became a great enthusiast. His feet no longer hurt him. He spent many an hour working out the steps and then rehearsing them with Mother. When they started to teach dancing, an atmosphere of tenseness eased from the house. Things seemed lighter again, more like the happy times before I was seven. From that time parental quarrels seemed to diminish, even disappear; I felt relieved.

By now I was finding a great deal of success in studies and was reading voraciously. I absorbed Treasure Island, living through every swashbuckling battle. Mike and I were steady visitors at the town library where kindly Mrs. Billings kept us supplied with favorite books. I felt like I was putting money in the bank when I returned a book to Mrs. Billings. Brushing aside a whisp of gray hair to raise her glasses, she beamed *her pleasure at seeing me again and carefully stamped my card, thus clearing my accounts for another couple weeks.*

A small town affords few places of escape. One of the favorite haunts was a forboding place down by the river. Our gang of the four musketeers—Dick, Jim, Mike and I—would sneak on down along the Sheyenne, cross a high railroad trestle, and settle in for the afternoon under the shade of the oak trees hanging out over the water. Sometimes we would go fishing, more often we headed for the cool shade where large, gnarled grapevines overhung the river. Each of us in turn would latch onto the longest vine and swing out towards the middle of the river. We never swung very far, but we felt daring to ride on out over the threatening stream down below. We were often exhausted by the mindless freedom of summer.

As I finished eighth grade my teacher, Sr. Berard, remarked how wonderful it was that Denny Kelsh, our Catholic neighbor, was the valedictorian that year at the public high school. I silently resolved then and there that I would achieve the same academic distinction in high school, which I did four years later. After I had given my valedictory address, a local farmer came into the drugstore and told Dad: "You know, your son would make a fine preacher." At our 20th anniversary of our graduation from high school, the planning committee invited me to give the talk again. Chagrined, at repeating the trite phrases of an 18-year-old, I repeated the performance. My friend Sharon said: "Now I can understand what you were talking about. It was way over my head 20 years ago."

High school was a painful time of waiting. I excelled in all my classes, loved math, general science, chemistry, biology, and Senior English. More often than not my academic interest depended on how well I liked the teacher. During these years I was painfully private. I had a few close friends, mostly those I had known in grade school. I escaped into studies be-

cause I experienced success and security there. But through it all I felt like a social klutz.

During my freshman year, my sister Cathy was born so I had plenty of chores around the house and was frequently called on to take charge when the folks were gone for an evening. They were still dancing frequently. When mother was pregnant with Cathy, a lady said: "Do you think you should be dancing when you're pregnant?" Mother retorted: "If I waited until I was not pregnant, I would never do anything!"

In addition to a cranky English teacher, the only event I remember about my sophomore year of high school was a trip to New Orleans for Mardi Gras with my folks and Mike. The Southern trip recalled memories of traveling together when we had moved West.

New Orleans was a great carnival. Each day the huge, loaded floats drifted down Canal Street and the pretty girls tossed out beads. The doubloons were not in vogue until four years later. But more exciting than the parade were the people who streamed in to stage their own Mardi Gras in the streets. I roamed the electrifying streets, sampled the praline candy, and snuck into the bars to feel the pulse of the crowd. At the end of every bar was a man with a soiled half-apron, schucking oysters out of the shell. Most of New Orleans is only a few feet above sea level, so the graves are all above ground— French style, with a lot of family mausoleums. Having read Dinner at Antoine's, *I was eager to eat there, but when we sampled the prices, we settled for its country cousin called Tujacques. I relished the chance to sip French coffee and munch a croissant. When we left New Orleans to head on along the Gulf Coast towards Mobile, it rained seven inches. With the warm rain these joyous memories sank into my mind. I remembered the peaceful, rainy walks in the winter at my aunt and uncle's ranch on the West Coast. I would not experience anything like New Orleans again until I went to Europe for studies 13 years later. I felt a breather from the*

*narrow confines of home and a chance to enjoy our little
family away from the daily tensions.*

*When we were in Louisiana, Archbishop Rummel of New
Orleans ordered the integration of all the Catholic schools
and caused a huge uproar. Headlines screamed the indigna-
tion. All the rest rooms were separate. Dining areas and buses
were segregated. Dad said, in his dogmatic way that often
irritated me: "It will take another 100 years to arrive at real
integration, just as it took 100 years since the Civil War to get
this far."*

*As we headed north, we passed through Boys' Town,
through the slightly green fields of winter wheat of Nebraska,
and on into the northland where once again snow covered the
road and the wind whipped along at the car and scattered the
birds foraging through the stubble fields. The bleak landscape framed my memories of the Mardi Gras, parades, gardens, and plantations.*

*We were all expected to have jobs. If we did not have one
elsewhere, we always had one at the drugstore, sacking the
horehound candy, dusting shelves, washing windows, scrub-
bing the terrazza floor, and finally clerking. Hours were ir-
regular when working for Dad. You could be called simply
when things got busy. So I felt fortunate when the Penney's
store manager asked Dad if I would available to work in the
clothing store.*

*I enjoyed the high-school dances or record hops, as we
called them. I could dance reasonably well since my folks,
who had started teaching ballroom dancing to adults, had
rounded up a group of us high school students to teach the
basics of fox trot, waltz, polka and jitterbug. Our tried-and-
true dance though was the Lisbon two-step, a halting shuffle
to the right, then a step to the left. At a dance the guys
grouped together in one area, mustering the courage to dance
with their favorite girl. The steadies just clung together.*

The formal invitational dances were more formidable. For

the Junior Prom I summoned up my courage to ask a girl
after prodding from Gloria and Ann, two stalwarts for Ann
Landers-style advice. They themselves were going steady and
were matronly in their security. When the Senior Prom rolled
around a year later, I determined whom I was going to ask,
had down all the right questions and answers and then when I
called, she refused. She wasn't going to go since her regular
boyfriend was out of town. In the end I went stag and spent a
miserable evening. That solitary night capsulized my painful
high-school years.

The bright spot in senior year was the new English teacher,
Mr. Andrews, a marvelous, Lincolnesque, gangly man of 25
who made music out of poetry and common sense out of
philosophy. He spellbound us, and for the first time my
unearthed talents for writing were mined and I found myself
delighting in a world of creativity that belied the drab yellow
bricks of the old school. Under my mother's tutelage I had
read voraciously throughout high school. When I was a freshman, she had placed The Citadel by A. J. Cronin in my hands
and I was hooked on books. That year in English with Mr.
Andrews I was a chrysalis which had finally burst its shell.

I was selected by Mr. Andrews for one of the leads in the
senior class play: Mortimer Garth. Mortimer was a young
English chap fresh out of Oxford who made life miserable for
everyone by his donnish mannerisms and abominable accent.
Besides murdering the American ear, he murdered his willful
uncle for his money. The part was deliciously villainous, and
I delighted in assuming his eccentricity. My stilted English accent betrayed its North Dakota roots, but by the end of seven
weeks I was living and breathing Mortimer Garth. Throughout the day I thought with an Oxford accent, and I felt a
jaunty air to my walk which mocked the gray days of a delayed springtime. The part called for me to smoke a pipe, but
we were not certain whether the superintendent would allow
it in the school. To prepare for the eventuality, I closeted my-

self in the bathroom to practice lighting up, puffing thought-fully, and exhaling manfully. The pipe was not allowed, but I was a hit and so was the cast—at least to ourselves, our friends and our parents. That is all who mattered; in Lisbon there was no one else.

When I graduated from high school in 1958, I was voted by the Senior Class as the quietest, the shyest, and the most likely to succeed. A "winner" in three categories.

When decision time for college arrived, I determined to go to either a Jesuit college or to St. John's, Collegeville. I had no direct encounters with the Jesuits, but from my reading in history, I was intrigued by their unbiquitous presence in politics, education, and the missions. I pored over catalogues from Gonzaga, Marquette, Fordham, Creighton, and Seattle University. At one point I was all set to go to St. John's; then, rather typically, my mother said: "Your dad thinks it would be better if you went to Gonzaga." At the time I did not discover why he thought so, but for me it was a toss-up anyway, so I chose Gonzaga.

Nobody in Lisbon had heard of the place before. The Catholic pastor recognized the name as being the patron of our parish, St. Aloysius Gonzaga. My relatives wondered how I could go so far away to school since they thought I was such a mother's boy. Mother and I had no such problems. We knew it was the best thing. Furthermore, I was already interested in a teaching order of priests. I was not ready yet to make a choice for priesthood, but I wanted to seek an alternative to being a country priest in North Dakota.

I was not disappointed in Gonzaga. I found the atmosphere exciting, even electric. My circle of friends had been restricted in high school; suddenly I was closer to more people than I had known before. Furthermore, the teachers were excellent, provocative and intelligent. I struggled through the first calculus course and the severe corrections of an English comp teacher; shortly I found my stride.

Philosophy, literature, and history were great liberating

forces. The Church was speaking in a brand new way to me. The Jesuits delved below the surface and opened up large, looming questions about our country piety. My enthusiasm was infectious, so my brother Mike also joined me. Two days before we were scheduled to leave, Dad called home from the drugstore: "if you boys can leave today, there's a salesman driving to Billings that you can catch a ride with." We leaped at the chance to save a few bucks and to forgo the tediousness of a long bus ride. My mother was upset with the abrupt departure. She needed time to absorb the change. "When you went to Gonzaga," she told me later, "I was so proud and grateful, but when Mike left I felt every one was leaving. Before you know it, there would be only Dad and me. I took out my frustration by being mad at Dad for two days." Perhaps she was a little more emotional than usual because she was pregnant again. My sister Ginny, the last of the nine of us, was born the following spring.

Years of joy. Years of pain. Engraved forever. Ignacio Silone said that a novelist uses the material of his first 12 years of life for all his creative work. In the summer of 1977 I glimpsed the past and tapped into its energy in a resourceful way. My own specters did not vanish in the act of recall, but they lost their power over me. I could absorb my own history. I could accept and appreciate my father, with gratitude, rather than a perplexing resentment. I gained perspective on my parents' struggles and especially their achievements. They had done the best they could, not in any minimal way. Mother challenged me to be the best I could; and Dad gave me an example of resolute integrity. I could accept them, and, therefore, myself.

Once I discharged the fear and anger from my system, I could see my dad as he was: kind, reserved, strong-minded, an ethical and generous man who was sometimes stubborn in his opinions. I found that I was very much like him.

That week in late July I wrote an article for the school

which was severely edited by the new president of the school.
I was ticked. I needed to confront him. Instead I talked over
my frustration with Zieverink. He commented: "People
don't learn much by being told what is wrong with them."
Later that evening the president invited me to join him at an
outdoor play. As we wandered through Washington Park,
near the rose gardens, he asked my opinion on several situations in the school. I was happier in my role as counselor than
I would have been as the confronter of his peccadilloes.

At the hospital we had been taught to express our anger. Z
added: "The process should have three steps. The first is to
recognize anger. The second to express it, and the third to
find out why you were angry. Unfortunately at the hospital,
the third step is neglected." He commented sagely: "In the
case of your anger over your article being edited, you were
acting out your anger, like an adolescent. Socially it doesn't
work too well. We will see if we can work around that step.
It also seems to me that you are ready now to be angry at
your father."

July 23, 1977. Whatever else mysticism might be, essential-
ly it is knowing the depths of one's soul in the light of God's
love who alone can accept me as I am. I have experienced a
few psychic phenomena, but I am no mystic. Safer ways of
arriving at the Lord's love exist; ecstasy is one of the more
deluding ways. It can lead to smugness, even despair, if psychological disintegration occurs. In the face of adversity,
one's faith can be strengthened. Graham Greene speaks of
"the kind of faith that issues from despair." The atheist and
prayerful person have much in common.

July 31, 1977. St. Ignatius Day. A look back at my retreat
two months ago: My anger ripped away a facade, helped me
to touch the Lord's love. I felt free. No longer was I bound to
a slavish following of events and orders. I carefully listened to
my own inspirations. I could see, hear, and interpret events
and not be driven by them. I did not need to prove myself to

the Lord, but rather to accept his call and respond the best I could. I was still anxious; I began taking stelazine again. Zieverink said it takes about three days for it to fill the system. He recommended taking it prophylactically or preventatively. We talked a bit about my mother. I commented: "My mother did a lot of things to please her own mother. It occurs from generation to generation. She told me once that when she wrote the book for her folks' 50th anniversary, she did not write it the way she really felt about everything, but rather the way she thought her parents would have wanted her to write it. There's some unfinished business that we could talk about on this subject," I said uncertainly.

"There always is. Psychological health is a lifelong process, but you are free enough now to do most of it on your own. The time may come when you need help again, but you have struggled through many issues and restructured your way of handling things."

August 3, 1977. I had two more days with Z. Leaving him was like changing parents. He had already made arrangements for a psychiatrist in Chicago to see me periodically. When I came into Z's office that day, I commented: "Your lamp light is out. Is that symbolic of something wrong?"

"I suppose it is. One of the staff members on the Ward had a personal emotional disturbance which was very distressing today."

August 5, 1977. Today was the last session. We summarized a few themes and reminisced about others. "It's too hard to be perfect," I sighed. "I hope I can practice what I've learned."

"You haven't just learned it like you would in a book. You have absorbed it into your skin. It's becoming a new way of reacting."

We talked about the transfer to Chicago and the new psychiatrist. Z concluded: "Very few people have been as sick as you were and are now as well as you are." Before we parted, I presented him with a gift I had been saving, a

Meerschaum pipe that I had bought five years before in Istanbul. Part of the turban was chipped and I had had to glue it together again. "You can see it's an image of me; my head is put together again."

"Thank you very much. I'm sure I'll enjoy it."

"It's probably too fancy to smoke while you're doing psychotherapy. The fierce head would stir up fantasies in your patients and transform the neutral atmosphere you have worked to establish in the room."

"You're right. You be sure to write." Just like my mother. But then he corrected himself: "At least be sure to write to say that you don't want to write."

I chuckled. I said goodbye with a lot of unexpressed feeling. I walked slowly down the steps, out of the dark waiting room and lingered briefly before the two apple trees. The pruning had done the job; a small crop of full-bodied apples clung to the trees. I felt I was seeing the burnt-orange, stucco house, the trim laurel hedge, and Mt. Hood in the distant haze for the first time. What happened to the 255 sessions with Zieverink in between?

December, 1982

I woke up and I was back in time. 7:56. Too bad Faulkner used that line first. Quentin section. That didn't leave much time for writing this morning. Flipped on the classical station. A Mozart string quartet playing a relentless, harmonious tune. Set the pace for the day. Reassessed my optimistic beginning for the new day when I poured orange juice over my raisin bran.

Our local curmudgeon, Harry, 76, was recovering now. Not as swiftly as before. Forty-one years at Prep takes its toll. He's as feisty as usual at breakfast, though none of his usual witticisms. Dom was excited about the lead article in the paper. They moved 18 Bighorn sheep from Hall Mountain, north of Spokane, down to the Blue Mountains by Walla Walla. Five rams and eight ewes from a flock of 70. Magnificent creatures. Dom's our poet-cowboy in the outdoors.

School buildings were quiet on this Saturday morning, just before Christmas. Cars and trucks would not roll in for grade school basketball for another hour.

"Father Nealen, your old classmate from the novitiate, was asking about you, Harry."

"They always want to know after you've been laid up for a few days in the hospital."

"I told him they pumped two more pints of vinegar into you and you were as good as new."

He chuckled at the half truth. "How's your book coming?"

"Chapter 11, coming up."

"Oh, don't say that! That's the bankruptcy chapter!"

"Bankruptcy came for me in Chapter 6. I've reorganized now, and it's going well."

"Keep it cheery. We've got enough grousing by ourselves."

Chapter Ten
THE DAILY STRUGGLE

So it was over. The intense sessions for two years with Zieverink were behind me. Somehow I felt the same intensity would continue in the future. It did not. My emotional life and reflective capacity tapered off fast once the initial phases of the new moves were over. Life slipped back to an even keel for the next couple of years. At first I had a hard time recognizing this new dimension of ordinariness. Something more should be happening. Choices should be sharper, insights deeper, and life should continue to be a searching struggle for coherence and meaning.

Chicago was to be painfully ordinary. On my way there in early September I stopped in Minnesota to see my parents. Retired for three years, they had built a new home where their cottage stood on the lake front. I was still sensitive to every nuance and I sifted conversations to find a grain of insight. One day as my mother pulled up the faded geraniums, which the frost had shriveled, we talked about their retirement.

She brushed back her graying blond hair with the back of her hand; she reminded me of Katharine Hepburn. "In the end all you have is your children. It is the only thing that lasts. I used to think Dad had the store, but now that's gone too."

"I think he's more interested in us than he used to be. He doesn't worry about where the next buck is coming from."

"He still fusses, but it's about the ordinary things, like laying in a winter's supply of wood or when Margaret and Tom are going to visit us."

Later that week I saw a rare side of Dad when my brother Joe called to say he had been hired to teach at the high school in our old home town of Lisbon. Dad was extremely happy that Joe landed the Lisbon job. He shed rare tears and his voice tremored with excitement. A few days later it looked like the job might fall through; I saw him get just as angry as he had been elated before. I realized more sharply the source of my fear at his anger. He loved each of his children, but most of his struggles were fought out on an interior level. About five years later in a moment of rare revelation, he said: "We love all of you very much, but you probably didn't always realize it."

Mother was more transparent. She said what she felt. I lived and breathed her openness so regularly that I rarely reflected on it. Like the weather, she was always there and I took for granted her loving nature.

The day before my folks drove me to Minneapolis-St. Paul, Mother and I were cleaning the last flower bed together. I ventured: "Mike and I were always competitive." I pulled out a clump of faded petunias.

"Yes, but you always stood by each other. When you entered the Jesuits, Mike said: 'They are getting a good man.' She added: "You sure surprised me when you entered."

"I'm surprised you were surprised. I always thought you expected it." It was easier to talk with her when she was occupied with ironing clothes, weeding a flower bed or such; otherwise she was up and away doing something. She could not relax until everything was in order.

When we said goodbye at the airport in St. Paul, I sensed a somewhat changed relationship toward my parents. The past struggles were slipping away and I could let go of them freely. I had to say goodbye to the past in order to welcome the present. I grieved a loss of the warmth of home and security. After a quick flight to Chicago, I arrived at the Jesuit theologate. I moved into a huge brown house on Woodlawn Avenue on the edge of the University of Chicago campus. I was only two blocks from the Reggenstein Library, the modern equivalent of the medieval cathedral in this academic community. My room was a pinched, ugly garret. I spent two days cleaning and repainting it.

As a precaution I took the El down to the loop and saw my new psychiatrist, one of the many that reach out like cranes along the El to pluck off the patients. I took an immediate distaste to his obsequious manner. Like a voiceless light fixture, he shone brightly, casting shadows over my gloom. He dipped his head to assert that he was listening. He reminded me of the weasel-faced psychiatrist who used to see Margot in Portland. His responses were dull and pointless. Casting away the last safety net after three visits, I stopped seeing him.

My course work in education at the University of Chicago was painfully boring. I wondered why I had ever made this patently absurd choice and looked for the nearest alternative. This struggle with the drab, academic life lasted for several weeks. One of my professors of education, who was retiring the next summer, said to a student: "You should go to another graduate school if you can because the University of Chicago's prime in education is over. It's resting on the laurels of old men." This advice confirmed my own assessment. And I chafed that I had not found this out before I arrived.

How does one give meaning to one's life? Or how does it become creative? Perhaps the residue of 37 years is the clay to mold a life—born anew, redeemed from the lack-lustre, molded to an unsung melody, strikingly right. Most of the time I felt my life floating away without a pause, without a rising, without a cresting, crashing breaker to cut the monotony—simply an ebbing away. Instinctively I knew it was easier not to probe the massive internal scar tissue that lay at the depths of my dreams.

In late December, Fr. Pat Stewart, the president of Gonzaga Prep in Spokane, invited me to apply for the job of principal. Surprisingly I did not leap at it. I clung to the notion—that was all it was by now—that I would somehow finish the doctorate. After a month of delay and struggling through fantasies of the future, I applied for the position.

I flew to Spokane for interviews. Since I was not concerned whether I got the job or not, I could perform without consequences, and I found the freedom exhilarating. When I arrived back at O'Hare airport in Chicago, I got on the bus to Hyde Park and a black passenger, a straggler, got on with me. He was intoxicated and flippant. He said to the driver: "Hey, man. Take me to the ghetto!" Then in his slurring, garrulous drawl: "When I was in California, I didn't see one cockroach. When I get back to my apartment, I'm going to sneak up, flip on the lights, surprise those little critters and say: 'Hey, fellows, I'm back!' " I too was definitely back.

Shortly after I returned, Pat Stewart called. I had the job. It was a great release. There was life after Chicago. My mind fastened on the possibilities of what I had seen at Prep; I could skirt the shadow boxing with my past.

In March I went to the Jesuit novitiate in St. Paul to spend a quiet (I hoped!) retreat. I took my theme from the psalmist's line: "Don't be anxious and watchful, for I am your God." I felt the need for healing and to drain away the anger towards God for having "allowed" the breakdown, especially during my retreat. I was also fearful that acute anxiety might occur again. Doug, the novice master, read from the Ignatian rules for the director of the retreat which calls for him to recreate with the retreatant or have someone else set aside to do so if the retreatant should need it. This authoritative comment from St. Ignatius freed me to pace myself and avoid my typical perfectionism during a retreat.

The city was emerging from winter. Bright rivulets sprang from the snow and glistened on the pavement. St. Paul was cleaner and sharper than Chicago. We had 77 inches of show that winter in Chicago. People did not even notice the seething frustration of coping with an unworkable city. An incident reported in the Chicago *Sun Times* capsulized the winter. A home owner had spent several hours shoveling the snow in front of his house in order to park his car, then he left two saw horses to guard the spot and drove off. When he returned that night, someone had parked in his spot. Infuriated, he hooked up his garden hose and for the next two hours caked the car with layer after layer of ice so that only a tow truck could release the ice-imprisoned intruder.

With great relief in June I left the sprawling unmanageable city of Chicago. It didn't work without Daley. I plunged in enthusiastically as principal of Gonzaga Prep in Spokane. From its founding in 1887 it had been a traditional Jesuit prep school for boys. Then in 1975 it had gone coed when the Holy Names Academy for girls closed. The Jesuits had been the major component of the faculty until about 1972 when an influx of lay teachers occurred with the decline of Jesuit numbers. Six years later some sorting out needed to be done to secure a solid, dedicated faculty. I recalled T. S. Eliot's line: "It's not the harvesting, but the planting that's important," and I dug in with new energy. After a relaxing summer of planning and preparation, I had an anxiety attack in mid-August because of the challenge of starting anew as principal. Within five or six hours I calmed down and was able to manage my day. I became aware of the undercurrents of emotion and how much I was investing in this new job.

I knew from the last three years that I was carried forward, kicking and squirming, to a knowledge of myself, to confronting my impulses, emotions, and memories. Because I was now more comfortable with my own identity, I could be more creative in facing the world around me.

Psychoanalysis cures the neurotic misery, Freud said, in order to introduce the patient to the common misery of life. To see such misery was to die to self, to die to neurosis in order to live a richer, apparently poorer, life.

In August Pope Paul VI died. While watching the solemn funeral Mass, I recalled the different times I had seen him in Rome in the Piazza at St. Peter's, at the Easter Mass, at the canonization of Edmund Campion and the English martyrs, at several audiences, as well as when I served his Mass at the Gesù church in Rome. He had not only held the nascent, reformed church together for 15 years but had led it with great spirit through the trials and exuberance following Vatican II. The funeral Mass was the end of an era of excitement and experimentation.

Spokane did not have the carnival spirit of Rome, nor the plainness of Chicago. It was manageable. My expectations were grounded in familiar, well-defined territory. I could avoid the pitfalls of trying to do everything myself and of isolating myself from supportive companions.

The first week of school went extraordinarily well. One faculty member told me I came across as "quiet and academic." The faculty liked my act, so far. Over the years so many people have told me that I am "academic" that I guess I must be. The warm welcome by the teachers was renewing during those first several weeks. I knew I needed the faculty's support. As Karl Rahner put it, my knowledge "is only a small island in a vast sea that has not been traveled." Though I was more interested in defending the island than in exploring the sea, I would need to forge an alliance with the rest of the faculty.

I had another anxiety attack in late November. As it came and went, I knew I could cope with severe anxiety; I gained confidence that I could manage stress and conflict.

After I had been principal for several months, the ordinary quality of the job became clear to me. The content would change from day to day, but a definite routine developed. I would wake from the world of dreams and enter a world of dreams-in-action. I shut off a persistent alarm and tried to catch that last fleeting dream.

Shaving is a ritual. A small machine making me presentable, scraping off the remnants of sleep to meet the day. Water, like a fresh baptism, brings me to life. I never make any resolves in those early moments of waking. Nor do I try to recall yesterday; usually the pains are foremost and most acute. Best forgotten.

Like Jerry Cobb, another Jesuit friend, I fluctuate between the optimism of Genesis, looking in my mirror and saying, "It is good," and the pessimism of looking in my mirror and saying, "Oh, no." Generally I cannot say, "It is good" until my first cup of coffee, the first of 12 or 15 for the day. My image of an office is of instantaneous injections of coffee, like intravenous feedings. Of course that dispenses with the sociability and flavor which are critical.

Breakfast is my coming-to-life period. One glass of orange juice, one bowl of raisin bran with milk and sugar, and a cup of coffee, of course. Beware of breaking the measured ritual. Reading the newspaper at breakfast always struck me as particularly backwards. How can I handle the world when I cannot even handle myself? Reduced to print and short headlines, however, even the biggest problem has its limits. At our house there is always a tension between the "readers" and the "skimmers." I want to skim the headlines and be off to work, but a few stubborn readers, often cigarette smokers to boot, are painstakingly memorizing the news. At such moments I am ready to part even with my coffee, to pour it slowly down their necks to speed them up and to wrestle the newspaper from them.

All this time I am steeling myself for the day's activities. My armor falls into place to deal with a grumpy teacher or an intractable student pushed forward by his angered parents. The first half hour is the worst. Fortunately the secretaries are cheery and punctual. I used to rush around finding the substitute teachers for the day. After several years of wretched beginnings of the day, I passed the job off to a secretary. Finally calm descends. I sit at my desk. The bells are about to ring everyone to their classroom; I say a prayer over the day. I realize, like the disciples on Mount Tabor, that it is good to be here. Although I do not comprehend what is going on, I'm ready to build some tent of permanency.

I sign a few letters that the secretary finished before I got to the office. I sign 25 certificates for the boys' basketball team. My signature appears on so many documents it will be worthless. First period goes well. I talk with a counselor or a teacher about a program. The English classes are over-crowded. We shoot for a goal of 28 maximum but rarely make it. That means more than 140 themes to correct for each assignment. The teachers in English are humanists, even toward me; they understand the dilemma of budgets and class sizes. We will do better next year. One year, in fact, I pitch in myself by taking on a Freshman English class to lighten the load of the Department. I creatively engage my students but find them disengaged. Yet I am surprised, often by the student who lingers after class, sometimes just to visit, sometimes to unfold a personal problem. Day-in, day-out they like my act. I think: "Wouldn't it be better just to teach five classes, be close to the students, grapple with their problems, get to know their families" and to close the book on the principal's job, this role as "glorified secretary?"

At the 10:30 a.m. coffee break, the teachers circle the wagons, engage in mutual support. Over coffee we interpret the events in our work lives. When the bell rings again, the teachers shift back to the solitariness of teaching. I continue to see visitors, fend off book salesmen and catch up on phone calls. How do we connect as a faculty? How can we build bridges of support? Surface the problems before they are cancerous, before the rancor sets in and I can no longer talk to a peer.

The longer I am at Prep the greater the stability. People are secure in a world of insecurity. They like their jobs; they are dedicated to Christian values, to being with kids and their hurts and joys. Yet they have lingering doubts. One teacher picked up on the title of *The Greening of America,* a slick analysis of the United States and spoke of the "The Graying of Gonzaga Prep." We grow old, we grow old. The questions remain: Am I doing the right thing? Even more pointedly: How long can I keep up the pace of this rat race?

My relationship with the teachers floats back and forth between accountability and encouragement. We have so many regulations that I like to emphasize encouragement, but my "closet Jansenism" creeps out to enforce the rules.

I enjoy organizing, solving a problem. I relish a well-run meeting, which is good, since I have so many of them. Ed Morton, who for years attended meeting after meeting, said that he felt he should start each one with an act of contrition because statistically he was bound to die in a meeting. I delight in teaching when I have a crack at it.

From experience I know I have to cross out part of my school calendar and give it to myself. I realize this most at the end of the day when I am taking a shower, perhaps the perfect prayer period. The hot, steaming water rushes over my body and I massage the back of my neck. All the tensions of the day wash down the drain. I try to see the day from God's perspective, trusting he will care for the hurting. I mull over the day; most of it flows away. I acknowledge God's closeness because it is God's work. "Yahweh I know you are near," and as Yeats says, "The unpurged images of day recede."

In February, 1979, I fired five teachers who I felt were unsuited for the school. By the time I had told the fifth one, I was in a daze. Torn between sympathy for their plight and a need to shore up the strength of the faculty, I was drained and exhausted.

Shortly after that I made my annual retreat. It was a time of peace and prayer, and I was confident I could pace myself in prayer so that my emotions did not soar out of hand.

One of the many things I had struggled with was my Jesuit identity. From the time I entered the order in 1961 the Jesuits had shared in the turmoil of the birth of a new church, which was rooted in the past but not a slave to it. An historically-minded church had superseded a rigid, institutional model that had remained largely unchanged for 400 years.

The 32nd General Congregation of the Jesuits in Rome in 1975 had attempted to describe this new Jesuit identity in the light of the traditional Jesuit charisms worked out in present apostolates.

The men at the Congregation were stretched to cover all the diversity of the Society's apostolic initiatives and commitments. The Jesuits were inserted into a world of rapid change. They were confused by tensions old and new in the Society and outside it. They were torn between the backward-looking and the forward-looking, between innovation and tradition, between development and liberation, between ideology and praxis, between capitalism and socialism, between the two sides of the Iron Curtain, between East and West.

In my prayer two ideas recurred from the 1975 breakdown retreat. I had been called to be a "discerner" and to be a "scribe." I still did not know what that meant, if anything. Perhaps nothing more than an interior desire to be fully Jesuit as Ignatius was. I also knew that this Ignatian way did not involve any heroics, but rather a daily fidelity to the Lord as he called me out step by step. My prayer now seemed saner, surer, more steadfast, and less of a search for glory. Once again I had entered into the retreat under stormy conditions but had glided to harbor.

The fall of my second year as principal I started teaching again with an Italian class for 27 students. The class was enthusiastic and I clowned around a bit in miming and acting out the language. One had to be exuberant to teach Italian.

I also saw Ingmar Bergman's, *Autumn Sonata* that fall, a film about a lifelong conflict between a mother and her daughter. One of the actors says: "Grown-ups are those who can handle their dreams and memories." Although some of my nightmares remained, I was sensing a new creativity in myself, a greater willingness to risk drawing strength from dreams and living with memories.

Risk was summarized for me by Gandhi. Someone had asked him: "If you had the power to change anything you could in the world, what would you change." Gandhi replied: "I would hope that I would have the power to give up the power." Deep down I was seeking the power that came with "perfect health."

That winter I was told that I would be a consultor of the province, one of the four key advisers to the provincial. I registered a shocked enthusiasm. I was eager to share in planning some of the directions of the province and of getting more involved with the life of the Society. I recalled Pascal's saying: "Job discovered love through the pain of suffering and Solomon also discovered the Lord through the pain of pleasure." I was ambitious enough to wish for honors, power, and position.

In February, 1980, four of us Jesuits started a small prayer group among ourselves. I was spurred on to it by a sense that my spiritual life was shallow. I was drying up in community and had no outlet for sharing or developing my spiritual life and of deepening my Jesuit identity. This desire struck a resonant chord with three others and so we met weekly to share our lives and prayer together.

In this prayer group I started to share what had occurred to me almost five years earlier. The wounds smarted when I talked about them. I was nervous, dry, and hesitant, but as I gingerly touched on the old pains, the sting was gone and I sensed a great relief, as well as support, coming from this intimate Jesuit group. An acute psychosis no longer seemed like such a painful, devastating experience, but more like a storm to pass through.

On May 18, 1980, Mt. St. Helens, 200 miles southwest of us, violently erupted and dumped a quarter inch of pumice on Spokane. We had just finished Baccalaureate Mass at St. Aloysius Church. The same day Fr. Pedro Arrupe, the Jesuit General, arrived in Spokane for a meeting of all the American provincials. By Wednesday the ash had settled, we had cleaned up the streets with fire hoses and Arrupe came to Prep to address a specially-invited group of teachers and benefactors. He talked of our ministry and the Society and said: "We make our paths by walking on them," showing the exploratory nature of the Society in recent years. This chartless route was one I had taken myself, but his saying it gave me a sense of accomplishment and purpose.

Later that week I confirmed with Joe Conwell, the tertian director, that I would be making tertianship, the final stage of formation in Jesuit training. For good reasons, I was apprehensive about the 30-day retreat that summer but looked forward to the other dimensions of the training, such as study of the Jesuit documents and history.

William Johnston in *Silent Music* mentions that latent psychotics should not practice Zen or certain prayer experiences. I was apprehensive about the 30-day retreat. I would need a keen sense of my emotional and prayer life and how they flowed into one another.

Johnston confirmed my experience that genuine prayer led to a deep appreciation for ordinary, sure-footed spirituality. My own strength did not matter. I had lived the ordinary for three years. "My power is made perfect in weakness. I will all the more gladly boast of my weaknesses that the power of Christ may rest upon me" (2 Cor. 12:7-9). By now I did not feel anxious about the faith sharing that would occur in tertianship. What I had to share was my weakness, which I hoped would reveal the action of Christ in me. He was my foolish boast. I prepared to move to Leo Martin House, the Spokane tertianship residence, for my final phase of formation and for the introduction to the oft-dreaded, now welcomed 30-day retreat.

Excerpt from The Catholic Sentinel, *Portland. Dec. 17, 1982.*

Jesuits Eye New Leader
Jesuits around the world will meet next September to elect a new superior general.
Major superiors of the 26,000 member order of priests and brothers throughout the world will select a successor to 75-year-old Father Pedro Arrupe, who has been incapacitated since suffering a stroke in August, 1981.
Jesuit Father Thomas Royce, Jesuit superior in Oregon will participate in the election with two representatives of the Oregon Province Jesuits.

"Gandhi" will leave Viewers Awe-struck
After an opening scene that shows the tragic end of Gandhi's life in 1948, the story is told in flashback. It begins in 1893 in South Africa with Mohandas K. Gandhi, a dapper lawyer with a Cambridge degree, riding in blissful ignornace in a first-class coach and attempting to open a discussion of the New Testament with a fearful black porter. . . .

Eugene Cobb, 62 of Gearhart died Dec. 8
at Portland Hospital
Surviving are his wife Peggy; sons Jesuit Father Gerald Cobb of Spokane, Neil of Albuquerque, N.M. and Jeffrey of Port-land; daughters Kathleen Cobb of Portland and Nancy Drendel of Lake Oswego; his mother Florence of King City; and four grandchildren.

Chapter Eleven
TERTIANSHIP—JULY- OCTOBER, 1980

I packed a couple of suitcases and took a load of books to the car for the five-minute trip to the tertian house near the Gonzaga University campus. At the end of June the hot sun seared the streets. Volcanic ash still lined the streets and blew from the rooftops.

Tertianship entailed a 30-day retreat and a study of the basic Jesuit documents and constitutions. The final plunge into the healing waters of Siloam. Broken and wounded, I needed healing; but I could live with brokenness too. I hoped for more. After Zieverink, my psyche was knitted together, but a residue of sore and tattered feelings remained. This had been a time of fasting from excitement, from challenge, from renewal. I had the hope now to peer into the darkness to seek out my soul, to face the leering specters, and to open the narrow confines of my imprisonment. I gathered my resources for the spiritual challenge ahead of me.

I lugged my suitcases up the cracked sidewalk to the porch. A gust of wind shook a spiral of dust from the roof gutters. "Dust thou art and to dust thou shalt return." I was entering into a Lenten season to prepare for the coming of the Lord. Joe, the tertian director, greeted me warmly at the screen door. Like a tonsured monk, he had a tuft of gray hair around the fringe of his head. His kind eyes gazed out from a fiercely prophetic face. Twenty years before he had been my guide to a Jesuit vocation at Gonzaga University. I was coming home to an old friend.

As I unpacked, I felt relief. I had arrived at the final probation in the Society. Five years ago I had despaired of ever making it. Then I questioned whether I would be allowed to continue as a Jesuit, let alone complete the final step of Jesuit formation in a 30-day retreat.

Weary from the rush of packing and moving, finishing up the last chores of school, I rested and prayed. God himself will set me free from the hunter's snare. Teach me to enter more deeply into the mystery of the church. Make my heart thirst for Christ, the fountain of living water. *Sphragis.* That is strange. I have not thought of that for years. Since the breakdown retreat five years ago. *Sphragis* had something to do with a seal or initiation. Was I inscribed, sealed and signed with the Lord? His possession? It affirmed a deep relationship, like a new baptism or outpouring of the Spirit. A death and new life.

Appropriate for psychic death. New life stirs within me and the source is unfathomable, lost in the eons of time and space. All I have is a broken spirit to offer. A living body as a holy sacrifice.

The ravens are clamorous and raucous. Sharp, painful images shriek for attention. Nothing is in focus, just a dull ennui like dreams in a fitful sleep. Squabbles, mistakes, arguments, I fumble for the right answers. Few seem pleased with the outcomes. Constant routine and no food for the soul to feast on. Where is the nourishment in the ordinary?

All the tertians have arrived: Pat, a lean, agile 30-year old who runs 10 miles a day; John from Missouri, a former high school principal, destined to be province treasurer; John, a resourceful brother from the Sioux Reservation in South Dakota. Hernando from Columbia, suffered much from political turmoil; Ted, an affable Oregon Jesuit, trying to lose weight and give up smoking; and Bob, another Oregonian, intense and genuine. Joe led the group. Twenty years had mellowed him, the edges were softer. He had harnessed his fierce temper so that our college nickname for him, "the fiery prophet," no longer seemed applicable. Joe Danel assisted him, mellowed now too, a 17-year veteran at Jesuit High.

We began our time in tertianship with a recollection of our

own personal faith history and where the Lord had touched us. I told my own broken story in two sessions. I steeled myself to relate the breakdown. I tried to be detailed. I wanted them to share the abandonment and despair. The second hospitalization after a tortuous year of recovery was the bottom. From there I caught a ray of the future and attacked the defenses and imprisonment with more vigor and determination. The years at Prep were easy to relate; they had a touch of growing success to them. At the end they applauded. It seemed like a movie that had come to a conclusion. Happiness and sorrow wrapped up in one continuous film. I felt relieved. I was less sensitive to the pain and more creative in capitalizing on my past. Listening to the woundedness and brokenness of the other Jesuits who had survived these 20 years was also healing and bonded us in fellowship.

For six weeks we studied Jesuit documents and tried to view the current Jesuit mission in the world. We struggled through the 1975 statements of General Congregation 32 and felt the disparity between the ideal of justice and the reality of oppression and poverty. Some of us argued that the ideal was a good goal, but not realizable in practice. We ran head-on into Joe, our fiery prophet once again, who had just returned from three months in South America and was steeped in the poverty and injustice he had seen. The sharp exchanges forced me out of my comfortable, one-sided administrative perspective.

The Thirty-Day Retreat
August 17 - September 16

The First Week

> Yahweh, You have searched my heart,
> And you know when I sit and when I stand
> Your hand is upon me protecting me from death,
> Keeping me from harm.

With apprehension I steeled myself for the thirty-day retreat. I expected no miracles; I was a realist. The purpose of the *Spiritual Exercises,* Ignatius said, is "to conquer oneself and to regulate one's life without determining oneself through any tendency that is disordered." Ignatius left more freedom to determine oneself than I felt, but he pinpointed the crux of the spiritual life by attacking disordered affections. I needed to be aware of them, not so much to curb them as to deal with them, in order to trim my sail, to tack or to veer to the winds blowing within me.

Childhood memories floated back to me: the haunting chant of the meadowlarks on a yellow-green North Dakota pasture, the coo-coo-wooing of the wood doves, the shimmering northern lights on a winter's night, and the power of an electric storm which I watched from the back porch. An unfathomable mystery. Raw power and sheer beauty flashing in the silver night. Tantalizing reminders of my mortality, loneliness and limitations. Could I say: "Yes" to the Lord without fear?

The intensity made me cautious. Like a confessor, I said to myself: "Be peaceful. Let it happen. Trust in the Lord. Place yourself in the Lord's guiding hand."

Expressing emotions comes hard for me. Some teachers at school think I am not taking clear enough stands or giving strong answers. Hesitancy comes from my lack of power or fear of power, a desire to be approved. Do not alienate anyone. Like the rich young man, I cling to security which prevents me from following the Lord and from trusting others.

Fear inhibits, causes hesitancy. Paralyzing. I recalled a potential disaster when we were novices on vacation at the ocean. Ten of us had waded through a cave along the beach just as the tide was starting to come in. The azure blue water swirled white around the rocks and sprayed mist against the walls of the little canyon that we waded out into. We clambered up a small ledge covered with seaweed; then each of us in turn scampered up the slippery, moss-covered embankment above the cave. Nine of us managed the feat, but one of the novices could not keep up his momentum and kept sliding down to the watery ledge again. Each time he attempted to crawl up, he slid down again. His fear mounted; shortly he was paralyzed. He could not go forward and it was no longer possible to go back because the tide had filled the entrance of the darkened cave. I carefully slid back down, supported him so that he could get up far enough to be pulled up by the others above us. I then clambered up the slippery embankment myself.

"Who am I that I should go to Pharaoh and lead the Israelites out of Egypt?" Paralysis. I'm dumb and slow of speech. The burning idealism of freedom saps my strength. The great inhibits the good, and I shrink from duty and from the front line. A burdensome weight oppresses me, but I am relatively happy building pyramids. Moving out of my security and possessions depresses me.

"At the favorable time I will answer you, on the day of salvation I wil help you." Don't do it alone.

Joe, the director, said: "The call to freedom is not always easy to answer; there are difficulties, ups and downs. The movement toward freedom is a passover, a journey from where we are to where God calls us. Passover is going out from our structural and personal egotism in order to be open to others and to God. It means walking, progressing, falling and rising again, never remaining stationary, passing from the slavery of sin to Christ and full humanity." Old Testament themes poured out of him, and a solemn twinkle lit his eyes.

I was losing control. I dreamed of a runaway train; I was a survivor along the tracks; I was building a fire with twigs, sticks and Russian magazines. At dawn I was drained, but rested. Could I sustain another 26 days of battling these tension demons?

The days went swiftly. Prayer a couple of time in the morn-

ing in my darkened room. A short walk around the block in
the bright sunlight.

On any day I sensed I was only five days from a psychosis.
Fatigue crept in around the edges. Hernando was called home
to Colombia the fifth day of the retreat because his brother
was shot and killed. A terrible violence blinds us to love and
drives God from the world. We groan in our travail, awaiting
our redemption. Poverty, weakness and the ugly face of
violence in Colombia, or wherever, shook me like death itself. Zieverink used to say: "It's O.K. to feel bad!" I wanted
to escape the ugliness of death.

I relaxed: let my prayer be simple. Be passive. Watch the
river flow and the candle burn. The clouds drifted overhead
and breezed on through the heat and blue sky. A leaf falls
and makes no sound and cracks only when it is walked on. A
swirl of volcanic ash is caught up in the wind and dances
down the street. A stranger drew near. Tall, flowing hair,
darkened in the sun. He sat alongside of me and I conversed
with him. We were high up on a hill in the middle of the
woods overlooking the vast expanse of the ocean above the
Nestucca River at the Jesuit Novitiate villa. He said quietly,
with strength: "We've been through a helluva lot together!"
With relief and tenderness, I felt understood and accepted.

"What are we supposed to do in this retreat?"

"Act justly, love tenderly, and walk humbly with your
God. It's between you and me. Right now, no one, no thing,
matters that much. You do not have to produce or prove anything." A deep silence passed swiftly. The quiet of the night
seeped through me restoring peace to my battered limbs and
strength coursed through me as through a person who has
finally recovered from a lingering illness.

The sixth day. God was bringing life where death abounded.
Along the ocean expanse of the Nestucca River, the Lord's
voice returned from the forest depths: "We have been together. We are together. We will be together."

After a period of prayer, I leafed through a series of Hopkins' poems which I found on the shelves in the tertian house library. I knew he had written a series of poems about his own tertianship experience. In one of them he described the uniqueness of each God-blessed creature and how each rang out a hymn of creation:

> As kingfishers catch fire, dragonflies draw flame;
> As tumbled over rim in roundy wells
> Stones ring; like each tucked string tells, each hung bell's
> Bow swing find tongue to fling out broad its name;
> Each mortal thing does one thing and the same:
> Deals out that being indoors each one dwells;
> Selves—goes itself, *myself* it speaks and spells,
> Crying what I do is me; for that I came.
>
> I say more: the just man justices;
> Keeps grace: that keeps all his goings graces,
> Acts in God's eye what in God's eye he is—
> Christ—for Christ plays in ten thousand places,
> Lovely in limb and lovely in eyes not his
> To the Father through the features of men's faces.

It captured my spirit and rang true, like the stone ringing round in the well. Each creature captured a moment of God's grace by fulfilling its destiny, its innermost self. The Lord called me to find that same destiny in myself.

Joe rocked forward slightly; his brown eyes agleam: "Perhaps the purpose of this retreat will be to see yourself as God sees you. As Hopkins put it for you—'Act in God's eyes what in God's eye you are.' "

Part of the retreat was to place one's personal sin before the Lord. The acknowledgment of sin is not self-hatred but self-acceptance. The Jesuit Congregation put it thus: "I am a sinner called to be a companion of Jesus." I drifted back to a huge Douglas fir stump on the hill above Nestucca, along the ocean. I am petulant, irritated when people tell me what I should do or how I should feel or especially when they interrupt my planned schedule.

"We know all about them. Let's talk about something else. How about your health!"

Thunder echoed in the distance. Was it a storm or just me? I sighed heavily. My health was a concern, but also a blind spot. One hope in this retreat was that I would feel totally well again. I could not ignore the question. "What is health for?" To praise, reverence and serve God. With poor health I was like the *anawim,* God's poor. But I prayed: "Lord, you could heal me if you would."

In my darkened room I could avoid these questions which escaped logic. I am not indifferent about my own health. I want to be completely well, not just surviving. It is a kind of power trip because if I have good health, I can do anything. Grasp it, clutch it, hang onto it. That is all I could do. Rush to examine and hold it. All I caught were the particles of dust shimmering in the morning light.

At the end of eight days, we had a "break day," an interlude in the retreat to help relieve some of the inherent intensity. Ted, Bob and I took a lunch to the Bowl and Pitcher, a natural rock formation along the Spokane River, surrounded by rapids and swirling waters. We were all relieved to be finished with the first week. As usual Ted regaled us with what had happened to him: "About the third day of the retreat I was feeling light-headed and then was suddenly very dizzy. The dizziness would not go away. I panicked, crawled around on all fours and tried to get my balance. The more I moved the more panicky I got. I thought: 'I'm having a breakdown just like Pat did in his retreat!' My anxiety and panic went on for three or four hours. My sinuses clogged up and I sneezed. Suddenly I realized I was getting a cold and it was probably affecting my ears and balance. I have never been so relieved to get a cold."

We crossed the rolling footbridge pitched across the rapids. A twisted metal cable, over a foot thick, secured the bridge to each side. The first week had been intense, but I had more resilience than I had thought. Bob had had a tormenting time that he did not explain. As we walked across the bridge, we had a spring in our feet as the swaying bridge rose up to meet us. I tossed a pine cone into the rapids and watched it swirl, twirl, then roll away in an undertow of current. I had learned, like a pilgrim, to walk with the Lord. The prayer of Zacharius, the father of John the Baptist, came to me: "In the tender compassion of our God the dawn from on high shall break upon us. . . ."

The Second Week

God comes to us in such a limited way, as a baby in a cave. He starts the way we all do—wailing and cold and loved by a tender mother and cared for by a responsible father. He is called to suffering and placed among the *anawim*. "Coming to your senses" means to be more incarnate, more human. The healing process meant seeing things for the first time. Kevin built some shelves from scratch for the laundry room; Gordon landscaped a backyard with petunias, marigold, delphinium, and geraniums. Vic carefully inlaid hundreds of different colored woods for his checkered wood boxes. These people carved out, shaped and sculpted the beauty of their own lives. In this second week the Lord was re-creating me: "Thou hast bound bones and veins in me, fastened me flesh." I felt remade after being torn asunder.

The life of Jesus from 12 to 30 years was uneventful, quiet and peaceful, except for a minor spat with his parents when he was twelve. This same tranquility was starting to pervade my body.

To remain *in* Jesus was to abide in his love, just as he remains in the Father. Further, we are empowered to be his disciples, which would mean the laying down of one's life. Our commission, the power we receive from the Lord, is tied to his laying down his life, to his being powerless, to accepting fully our human state. By laying aside my yen for power and my search for glory I could be with Christ.

Along the river, the weeds along the bank were dry and brittle. A few thistle bundles rolled in the breeze, but a line of green carpet fringed the flowing river. From the river Jordan to the Sermon on the Mount, the focus is on Jesus who is poor in spirit, gentle and persecuted. He is the parable of God.

After 16 days of an intensive retreat, these were ordinary days. I dwelt on the life of Jesus. Inner healing was going on at a deeper level, like a wick burning down within the core of the candle without visible flame, only an interior glow. The fire of the divine holiness glowed within me, without flame, without heat, but with a transforming power, kindled by aspiration. This uneventful aspect of the retreat was the most significant feature of the whole 30 days. In retrospect, it appears as my reception of the Lord working in the depths and my willingness to accept a certain plainness in prayer, a willingness to accept the Chicagos in my life. It was His work not mine which made all the difference. Prayerful people might describe this non-dramatic, but profound, prayer as a flameless fire or a cloud of unknowing. After 21 days of retreat, we took a second break.

The break furnished a pause to glance back at some previous retreats. My interior conversion began with wild Bill and his crazy parrot in 1971. The shared retreat at Galloro, Italy, prior to ordination, was a quickening of the flame. The volcanic explosion—my breakdown during the retreat in 1975—was both set back and advance. The psychosis, profound death, forced me to reconstruct everything from the ground up. I had to question everything. To discard outmoded structures and destructive habits and gradually to pray, live, and love in a new way. I accepted my personal history, which became a source of nourishment and hope. I was not abandoned. Others were there to help. Most of all I tapped deep within my being and found strength and inner resolve that had been obscured by fear and by desire to be accepted by everyone. I was accepted by God. That was enough.

Since the reforms in the 60's, provincials and superiors had become more responsive to the religious experience of each Jesuit. Real spiritual goverance was taking place on an individual level. Communitarian discernment was still a long way off because ordinary community living was sterile and routine. Jesuits sensed malaise, that something needed to be done; too often the "good" houses looked back to the old models for community renewal; a good table, a sense of hospitality, a strong rector who cared for the men, and a polite grace and a gentlemanliness which did not ask probing questions and kept a safe distance from others.

Despite the nostalgia for an irretrievable past, steady attempts at communal sharing—some mandated by the provincial, others arising spontaneously from the troops—were shaping the new Jesuits. More were joining shared-prayer groups or celebrating Mass together daily. A growing comfortableness in faith sharing was leading to a respect and interest in discovering the history of the province, tapping the wisdom of the older members, and appreciating the ideals of the young.

I paused in my reflections. It was getting late. Tomorrow was another day of retreat. I was about to start the passion of Jesus. Death and dying. Death to the old, so that life might abound. Would my stance be anger and bewilderment or acceptance and forgiveness? I heard Teddy come in and lumber up the steps to the room next door. His 250 pounds produced a solid tread. I to bed.

The Third Week

We considered the Last Supper, the Agony in the Garden, and the Death of Jesus. I was still struggling with thoughts about my health. Joe's room looked like my desk at home—a disorderly array in which he knew where to put his hand on most anything. As I explained my struggles, he said: "The disciples didn't do all that well either in entering into the passion of Jesus."

As in past retreats, I listened to classical music. The opening of Handel's "Messiah." "Comfort, comfort ye my people," touched my wounds. The solace of the First Week returned to me, thoughts of the "beloved Son," the transfiguring experience of the apostles. But the glory of Christ was obscured by the shadows of the Garden. These five days on the Passion went on forever and a heaviness enveloped me. I recalled past Holy Week services. In our home parish we used to have a vigil from the end of Holy Thursday services until Good Friday services. The Howells signed up for an hour of prayer; it always seemed to be about three o'clock in the morning. "We're closer to church and can get there easier," my mother instructed us.

"Will it ever end?" The presence of the Lord in the supper vanished and gave way to a raw violence and unnerving emptiness. I sorrowed and grieved without emotion or tears, and I thought it was easier to suffer through my own pain than through someone else's. I wanted to run, though chose to follow the pain in Gethsemane, the mental and physical anguish, and waited for the night to pass.

Good Friday had always been brighter because we usually raked the lawn and cleaned up the flower beds. Buds of spring were bursting and the warmed earth burgeoned with fresh sprouts. The hard, frozen earth yielded under the gentle blue skies of spring.

For our sake Christ was obedient, accepting even death on a cross.

Along the river the weeds thickened and burrs clung to my stockings. I should have worn boots. "It is accomplished." Could I drink the cup or even hold it waveringly in my hands? I reached the bend in the river where the bridge crosses. I pulled out some of the thornier burrs in my socks and walked across the bridge. It was tamer on this side of the river, close to the old hobo jungle.

The Fourth Week

These struggles with pain faded. With the Resurrection appearances, I felt I should be present to the Lord in a different way, but I felt unsure of myself. What was I called to do? Our unity as tertian retreatants grew in our silent exchanges. I shared the confusion, doubt and finally peace of the disciples rather than the joy and triumph of Christ.

Mary was among the first to recognize the Risen Lord. She was among the *anawim* and thus among the apostles expecting the Holy Spirit. She had been the first to be overpowered by the Spirit and had spent her lifetime listening to the Spirit and treasuring the words of her Son—an upsetting experience which led to peace and understanding.

A disheveled railroad tramp shuffled up and offered me a drink. "No thanks. I'm just out for a walk."

"I just came through Montana. There's already snow there. Cold as hell."

"Where are you going for the winter?"

"Oh, I winter here. Spokane's a good place for the winter. There's always food. People are decent."

"That's good. I like to travel too, but I don't have your courage to ride the rails."

"There's nothing to it. You just have to have patience." He curled up against a log in the sun; I kept on walking along the river.

Christmas, 1982

It lasted for a week. Swings of emotion and a cascade of events. On Christmas eve I drove to Prosser to my brother Bill and Lynette's orchard farm. Nursed a dreadful cold for two days. Planned to help Bill prune the cherry trees, but my head was swimming in phlegm. A boisterous family Christmas. I concelebrated the Christmas liturgy with the local pastor. At dawn the kids were racing around eager to open their packages. Later we cleared some brush along the river bank.

The day after Christmas I said goodbye, hugged the kids and left in the chill morning. I hadn't shaken my weariness from school and the strata of fatigue that remained. I needed air, rest and exercise to unwind. When I reached the Columbia Gorge at the Dalles, my head cleared; the Oregon air was therapeutic for my lingering cold.

Several Jesuits were holding a reunion at Loyola Retreat House. We could not get together unless we had a meeting. So we hobnobbed for two days on the theme of Jesuit Spirituality. Fraternal reunion, sparkling conversations and old friends were the main features. Peter, the young pastor of the downtown chapel, said: "My brother Bob is in town. Would you want to come down for a get-together later this evening." Bob, my retreat director in 1975, had left the Society the year before and was recently married. That evening seven of us gathered in the upper room of the downtown chapel, a parish center for the down and out, next door to the Star Theatre on Burnside. Bob was relaxed, subdued, and joyful as we listened to Jack, who was back from leading the first half of a peace pilgrimage to Bethlehem.

Peter explained what had happened at the chapel at Christmas. "Salvation comes through beauty, so for Christmas we had two violins and a beautiful set of carols. We tried it at Midnight Mass. I'm not certain it's the right thing to do in this Skid Row neighborhood. People are afraid to come out. But they came and they enjoyed it."

Christmas, 1982, had come for me too. Bob and I walked down the street together. We said goodbye; I departed into the starry night of Burnside.

Chapter Twelve
REDUCING THE STORM TO A WHISPER

I was grateful I had survived the retreat. It had been en-
riching, prayerful. As though I had emerged from a de-tox
center, I drank less coffee, relaxed, and slept better. After a
final round of faith sharing, the formal part of tertianship
finished for me. Two tertians went off to the Alaskan missions for a couple of months, another worked on the Skid
Row of Tacoma, another headed for an Indian mission in
Omak. Before returning to the high school for my third year,
1980-81, as principal, I took a week's vacation on the Coast.

I joined up with Bob, the close friend who had directed my
retreat when I had had the breakdown. We were going to
spend five days at his uncle's beach place on Whidby Island
in the Puget Sound. We eased our car onto the ferry just
before the churning ship slid away from the dock. The ferry
rolled away from the shore and surged across the bay to the
darkening island.

Bob had just finished three troubled years as rector at
Bellarmine Prep in Tacoma. His own kindness got in the way
of his need to be assertive as a superior. I told him that when
he said "No," some people heard, "Maybe," and when he
said, "Maybe," the same people heard, "Yes."

I tossed a pebble into the bay. "My tertianship retreat was
a time of great healing. It was as if all the debris of the breakdown retreat were dredged up and absorbed. I was retracing
each event and was freed of the stormy fear and anger."

"I never told you what happened to me when Jim and I
took you to the hospital," Bob said. "I was terribly frightened and concerned for you. After we left you, Jim and I
drove over to the Curia so Jim could tell the provincial what
had happened. Then I collapsed from emotional exhaustion.
I called Gordon and was speechless with grief. A long silent

sob hung on the line. Finally I said: 'What have I done to my friend?' Gordon said: 'Just be grateful you were there to let him down gently.' "

"I would never have made it without you, Bob. Your support saved my life. I would have gone completely berserk without you." We walked back to the house. The sun was setting over the rippling water of the bay.

That night I dreamed I was moving back into a huge old mansion. I went down three flights of stairs to the living room. All the walls were filled with frescoes. Some parts of the frescoes, those being restored, protruded from the wall. My mother was admiring the new carpet. "It wasn't here when we lived here before. This used to be your Uncle John's house." I felt good about the renovation.

Two days later I was sitting on the long davenport before the window gazing out at the surf and tide rolling in the breeze. *My creativity needs an outlet. I could write what has been happening to me. All this faith sharing, personal history and prayer is leading to something. My breakdown and hospitalization are now separate from me, distant and manageable moments. I am different in a different setting.*

The writing came easily and swiftly. I sketched out a short synopsis of my breakdown and its build-up. Time had winnowed the events to some memorable kernels and cast out the chaff. The closer I got to the present the less coherent the story became. That night in another dream a Jesuit chided me for triumphalism: "All you talk about is yourself." I let it sink in without resentment as if I were learning something about myself that I had never seen.

A true spirituality, I knew, would accept our human lot in all its poverty and weakness. Jesus expressed his love for the Father by accepting his own humanity to the full. Through the acceptance of his human destiny, Jesus was made perfect.

When the ferry docked on the mainland, we bade each other farewell. He was headed to California for "R and R."

I thanked Bob for everything he had done for me—far more than he would ever know, or that I could express.

My spiritual healing was soon tested by events at school. They would stretch my psychic security beyond the comfortable limits I had newly established. After a three-months' absence from school, I had a lot of catching up to do. I had not been able, naturally, to keep in touch with teachers and the normal events of the school. Some resentment at my absence was building which I was oblivious to.

At the end of February, the provincial assistant for education, Joe, visited the school and got an earful. He received complaints from teachers about my lack of responsiveness and indecisiveness. Young teachers were left to drift and the school did not have a clear direction. Too many projects got in the way of a genuine care for people. I felt fatigued by trying to catch up on my normal work, so I was not receptive to this criticism and felt the expectations of doing tertianship and continuing as principal were unrealistic. Discouraged, I resented the lack of understanding. However, the criticism also tapped into some latent energy reserve because I dug in with renewed efforts to be more responsive to the immediate needs of the teachers. The daily routine eventually re-invigorated me.

In February, 1981, I returned to Portland for an eight-day retreat at the novitiate; it was to be the summing up of tertianship. I was still battling disorders of my own making. The theme of intimacy with the Lord recurred and confirmed the 30-day retreat. Acceptance came with my full identity as a person, a sinner and a Jesuit priest. The Lord was leading me out of the years of personal chaos to a new vision and synthesis. He was uprooting my comfortable assumptions about my competence and questioning my accustomed ways. I could no longer build pyramids.

Though I felt beleaguered at the school, and I could not regularly confront conflict, these barbs were minor compared to the destruction of selfhood I had felt six years before. Whenever I was touched in a vulnerable spot, my resistance flared up. I wanted to be in control to reduce my fears, but was beginning to realize that control was not so important as responsiveness to a problem, compassion towards people, and generosity with my time.

Looking back over the six-year period, I knew I had weathered the storm. The initial exodus was over. The pain was with me, yet behind me. The Lord was present through it all, through the fear and trembling, through the acute, agonizing anxiety, through the growth and aimless wandering and grumbling.

My ship had finally come into port after a violent storm. The tidal-wave breakdown created a new beachfront. After the tortuous years of recovery, a calm came to me. The interior storm subsided, though flotsam and jetsam continued to wash up on the shore. The whisper of the Lord came unexpectedly. I had been used to the mighty wind that tore the mountains and to the earthquake of my own emotions.

March, 1983

A stream of student cars are negotiating the traffic and turns. I proofread the Prep Newsletter: three National Merit semi-finalists, soccer has a good season, students are working at Shriners' Hospital, fund drive is launched for fine arts center and gym. No teachers absent today. A relief. First bell rings and a flurry of kids race for the doors. Only a few stragglers today. I visit a first-period religion class taught by Dennis on "The Problem of God." He skillfully takes the students through some of the questions on God that Freud and Feuerbach had raised. "God is a primitive projection or a wish fulfillment." Students struggle with the dilemma and their own projections. "A person's being conscious of God is simply his being conscious of himself. God is a person's primitive way of discovering his own potential." Students weigh the pro's and con's of the arguments. Dennis does not let them off the hook.

Checked back with the secretary. Three phone calls to return. A parent wants his not-so-sharp daughter admitted to Honors English. A college teacher, he wants to make sure his daughter is challenged. The other calls are more pleasant. Fran is organizing a parent tutoring program. We have seven mothers lined up to start the program. The third call is to Peter, the Jesuit academic vice president at Gonzaga University. The University has not been recognizing the advanced placement scores our seniors received. Peter clarifies a few points. Quite helpful. I have some coffee.

Pep con for the student body. Not my favorite activity, but the students rally once more to the battle cry of one more basketball victory, a rousing band number, a crazy skit and fancy footwork by pretty cheerleaders. A teacher sees me about early dismissal for the wrestling team. The phone rings four different times. The treasurer has a question. The president wants to see me in his office when I am free. Another

mother volunteered for the tutoring program. The city plan-
ning commission called about a hearing on a throughway on
the bottom part of our soccer field. Gave the letter to the
secretary. She's fantastic. She runs the office. A sign on her
desk says: "Do you want to see the person in charge? Or do
you want to see the person who knows what's going on?"
The president wants my advice on whether we should readmit
Tom, a student who had been expelled for three offenses of
drug abuse. "His parents say he's squared away and still
wants to graduate."

"Let's wait until the fall. Then if he's in good shape, ac-
cept him on probation. He should see Terry once a week for
counseling." Time for coffee.

The bell rang. With a sheaf of papers, I headed for a math
class that Mark was teaching. A lively, young department
head, who set high standards for staffing his department. He
was a dynamo in the classroom. I gave my notes to the secre-
tary. She smiled as she picked up my hieroglyphics. Math was
the hardest class to decipher.

A scholastic saw me for spiritual direction. My listening
skills were not the greatest in the middle of the day. My mind
was on the office. I needed a hot shower to drain away the
tension. My psychiatric sessions with Zieverink furnished a
backdrop for spiritual direction. I knew what was going on
and what to probe beneath the surface.

Had to catch a flight out to Portland for a meeting tomor-
row. Packed in five minutes, grabbed my ticket and Fr.
Adams drove me to Spokane Airport. Great time to unwind.
I looked forward to these meetings with the provincial and
other consultors. It was easier to solve someone else's prob-
lems rather than address my own. As the plane dipped for
landing I saw the freeway in the distance winding around
Providence Hospital. It was a friendly sight.

EPILOGUE

November, 1981
I sent the first several chapters of a draft of this book to Dr.
Bill Zieverink to read. The material covered the period from
Rome to my release from the hospital, 1971-1975. When I
saw him in November, he had already finished five years as
the director of psychiatric services at Providence Hospital
in Portland. We met in his office—not the vine-covered,
neutral, stucco house, but the high-powered, energy-charged
office in the hospital. After we greeted each other, he started
glancing through the rough manuscript and musing over various passages. He said: "Your greatest line for me describes our
first meeting. You described me and then concluded: 'He
seemed competent.' Period!" He chuckled at the terseness.

"A lot of that will be developed as we go along. Do you
mind if I tape our conversation."

"Not at all. Here's a recorder on my desk. When I read
this, I found it really good. There's a good glow, feeling and
genuineness about it."

"I'm glad you like it. I must say it's easier to write about
than to go through it."

"What impressed me about reading this is how much more
you have done since we stopped treatment in terms of taking
others' insights and readings and integrating them into your
understanding of how people work. That's why this is so rich
compared to a sterile narrative of events."

"I had difficulty in writing this section because I didn't
want to give the punch lines away."

"It's true!"

"My 30-day retreat in September, 1981, will be the climax
of the story. My tentative title is "Memories, Dreams and
Retreats," very Jungian. When I get into my sessions with
you, I will use a flashback technique to pre-1971 and cor-
relate that with present insights."

He stuffed his pipe, stoked the furnace and started reading again. "You have little epigrammatic statements that are very salient and insightful."

He read from the text: "I experienced Christ as a personal friend . . . celibate life is not possible without an affective prayer life and personal relationship to Christ." "That's absolutely true and overlooked. It is hard to convey the necessity of having an emotional relationship with God—as a communication. What kind of life does one have if one is celibate and doesn't have an emotional life with God?"

"Do you think the story is too revealing, too personal to be published?"

He drew on his pipe: "It seems like a remarkably good balance of religious biographical style with personal content and personal issues. The reader knows it's for real. It is couched in classical theological context as a vehicle, but it is also emotionally rich because it is personal. This combination is rather unusual. Usually these biographies are very dry or else soupy confessions. You have a good balance. The question remains: 'How come?' Why did you have a psychotic break? It remains an unanswered question."

"We never did finger the precise reason."

"I don't think anyone can answer that question. You came into this setting with conflicts and anxieties, but nothing stands out as *the* reason."

"Is that somewhat typical of a psychotic break?"

"Yes. Most people would like to put their finger on some cause. People are too complicated. I mean, I think it's multi-causal."

"I do point to Molokai and to some tensions at Jesuit High."

"Yes, that's fine. You had all that going on. But why should that add up to a psychosis? I think there is a confluence of life events and then some biological event is present at the age of 35 that was not there, say, at the age of 32, or at 40. Biologically you continuously change. Most people would like to say: 'This and this and this happened to poor ol' Pat and he fell apart.' "

"During my first six months of our sessions, I kept trying to find a reason and the retreat thing kept coming up as causal and that reflection precipitated further anxiety and concern."

"How could a retreat, which is good, cause this terrible event?"

"I kept saying, How could God let this happen to me? It caused a lot of spiritual anguish."

"Are you going to get into that? Because that is not a unique question."

"That is still an unresolved question that I need to come to grips with. I am not certain I can do it except through writing about it."

"I contend that is another way of stating the problem of evil. I don't know what it is about you Jesuits, but every one of you is hung up on it."

"I allude to that by the quotation from Job."

"What does Job say?"

"It's a mystery. You don't knock your head against a mystery trying to solve it. You accept it, reverence it and go on living."

"Boy, if anyone agrees with that it's me! But an awful lot of religious people are utterly beset with the paradox of how a good God could let this happen."

"It is how we deal with evil, death, depression, misery, hunger."

"Exactly."

"I don't think there is a very good way of dealing with all that in a normal rational system. Living with it comes down to a sense of compassion and acceptance and going on from there. As you used to say so often: 'Things just aren't fair.' "

"Right Who said it was fair? But where were you ten years ago on all these things?"

"I accepted it rationally but not emotionally. Ideas were there, but they didn't have a gut basis."

"Why? This event of the breakdown flooded you with emotion, and you were overwhelmed, and then you came back together again. You got a better understanding through psychotherapy and you've gone on from there. So that you're a lot better off today than even before the breakdown. It is a real good outcome. It is not the common outcome. The pathway of tightness in your chest and continuing anxiety just gets narrower and narrower. Your life could have become more and more restricted and defensive. Then it is an ever-increasing job just to maintain control."

"I was liberated by this event."

"But that's not the usual outcome. It can be very frightening. Just before I saw you, I was talking about a new director of a program for our chronically ill. We need someone who has a deep sensitivity for what it means to never get better. I mean, can you imagine being like you were in the hospital for a month—*always*?"

"Terrible."

"When I was in training, I had a hard time getting in touch with that. It is terrible."

"It is living out of despair. At least I always had the hope of getting out of here."

"You had this incredible explosion of emotions followed by several years of integration of feelings and thoughts. What blocked this integration before the breakdown? You took that gigantic bolus of feeling one piece at a time, chewed it and swallowed it."

"Like castor oil!"

"Right. You finally got it back inside yourself."

"Writing has also been an integrative process. I feel better now than I have ever felt. There have been stages all along the way that I have said this. I don't know when I am going to stop saying it. I suspect fairly soon."

"Why was it that you tended to rely so heavily on intellectualization and the rational? I mean, I don't know. We
haven't talked much about that."

"I was successful in studies. Certainly in high school I
could bury myself in my books, and at the same time I didn't
really gain much reward for emotional expression."

"Do you think in your home, growing up, that's an ac-
curate statement? Sex and aggression are the two things
most people have a great deal of trouble with. They are the
unresolved conflicts of adolescence often enough. One
suspects that in your upbringing there wasn't the opportunity
to deal with these primary emotional forces in an open,
constructive way."

"I'd say sex wasn't talked about, and I didn't really deal
with that very well in high school. I never developed a close
relationship with a girl. Aggression, getting angry, was not
acceptable and because of a few parental explosions I felt
upset with any anger."

"Every profession has a certain self-selection process. How
many of your colleagues in the Society of Jesus have these
same handicaps?"

"Is that a rhetorical question too?"

"I am sort of baiting the audience here! One would suspect, certainly in the Jesuits with their high degree of in-
telligence, a self-selection of those traits or styles which
would be rewarded. Certainly when I was at a Jesuit high
school at St. Xavier's, Cincinnati, and a Jesuit college at Holy
Cross, the intellectual, the bright, smart and witty were way
up there. But emotional and social skills were secondary."

"James Joyce had some devastating caricatures of Jesuits
who were all mind and intellect and had sterile souls. The
intellectual life and wittiness of Jesuits certainly appealed
to me."

"O.K. That means a lot of your colleagues risk psychosomatic symptoms—tight chest, ulcers, headaches."

"Heart attacks at an early age and alcoholism later on."

"But how do you reconcile this intellectualization with what you described as an affective prayer life? And I suspect they have a lot of trouble because they sense their prayer life is somewhat sterile and ideally their prayer life should be the most vibrant part of their life. What do they do?"

"Well, there's a close relationship between your prayer life and your other affective relationships. One feeds the other. So if you are a bastard in community, you are probably a bastard in prayer!"

He absorbed this hyperbole, glanced down at the manuscript once more and said: "So what are you going to do with this book of yours? How long will it be?"

"I think about 150-200 pages. I hope to publish it. What do you feel about being named directly in this?"

"Oh, that's fine."

"You'll see that I'll be putting more quotes in your mouth as I go along in treatment."

"As I become more competent!"

"Yes! As you become more competent and insightful!"

"This book is like a mirror of who you are now—a balance of feelings and thoughts. A nice interplay of detail, intellectually, theologically sophisticated and simultaneously personal."

"Sometimes I wish I were reading this book about someone else."

He went back to reading and mumbling to himself. "Here's August 9, 1975, in the hospital. 'What is sainthood?' Golly, there's a lot of stuff here. You say you got this letter from your mother. How much is contained in that one page!"

"The most difficult part of writing is dealing with my folks."

His face lit up and he said warmly: "My advice is you should be charitable."

"Our relationships have improved dramatically."

"Isn't it amazing how as we get older, our parents mature so much."

I added ironically: "They know so much more at 65 than they did at 40! There are a number of things about my dad that I think will soften any earlier harshness I may have had. We have built a good relationship since I became an adult. When I was home in July, my mother said something that struck me: 'Why are you so much better now? You just seem terrific!' I wasn't up to telling her then. I felt like saying: 'Read my book.' "

"See the movie. The feelings and relationships we have with our parents are the most profound and, therefore, the most upsetting. Parents always do the best they can. It may not have been the best for you, but it was the best they were able for who they were at that time. As one gets older, one is humbled by how little we are able to do about anything." He added reflectively: "You have made such a remarkable improvement that . . . ."

"It was a partnership. You played a huge role in it."

"I started to say, it gives me a real sense of fulfillment professionally. You can work just as hard with many people and no matter what you do they don't get better. It's the same with parenthood. You can be the best parent in the world, and gradually it dawns on you that this child has come into the world with a lot of things pre-set. This writing project can be enormously rewarding not only to you, but also to your colleagues. The Society has had a lot of difficulty providing precisely this intellectual and emotional integration."

"There's a huge waste, a disease, and it can be a communal disease. A psychological crippling of resources."

"It is a tragedy, because the Society has an enormous collection of talent that is hobbled emotionally."

"I can quote you?"

"I think the tape ran out or I better shut up!"

We finished our session. I noticed he no longer had his

beard and was graying at the temples. The tremendous energy was still there, even more alive in this hospital office.

I heard him without narrowing our relationship to my own needs. He radiated care, interest, and energy.

As the plane roared into the air, it swerved to the northeast over the Cascade range north of the Columbia Gorge. We flew within a few thousand feet of Mt. St. Helens. I gazed out the narrow window into the devastated crater. A small dome, the size of a football stadium, was gradually rebuilding. A purple haze of ash and steam flowed westward to the setting sun.

I met Bill Zieverink instead of my enormous projections. He refused to meet my seductive need to be cared for which colored, often poisoned, my other relationships.

Retreats had been the crucible to purify the dross of my imagination, but I had made them magical, often expecting the director to divine what I feared to fathom.

Andre Malraux in his memoirs relates how he visited an old priest and asked him: "Father, after hearing so many confessions after all these years, what reflections do you have? The old priest thought for several moments and then replied: People are not as happy as they seem, and there are very few adults." People live out their childish fantasies over and over again. These childish patterns set the stage for an unhappy future. As controlling images, they cause a person to fall into the same destructive relationships over and over again. Sometimes their dreams come true; sometimes they are shattered. But there is little freedom.

I had worked through who I was and had experienced paralysis and numbness when my dream-world shattered. Reality poured in like a terrible deluge. In the journey out of this chaos I was painfully vulnerable because it was uncharted and unpredictable. I had to shed old patterns and security.

The healing came as a gift. Friends converged to help me

build new relationships and struggle with old ones. Now I could begin to love others in intimacy.

   The fog was breaking up as the plane circled Spokane to face the westerly winds for landing.

The plane gracefully touched ground and taxied up to the landing gate. I was home again. I gathered my luggage and bumped on out through the narrow aisle. Outside the terminal a little car edged forward and kindly Fr. Adams peered out and warmly called out: "Welcome home, Pat. How was the trip?"